Reminiscences of the Campaign of 1814, on the Niagara Frontier

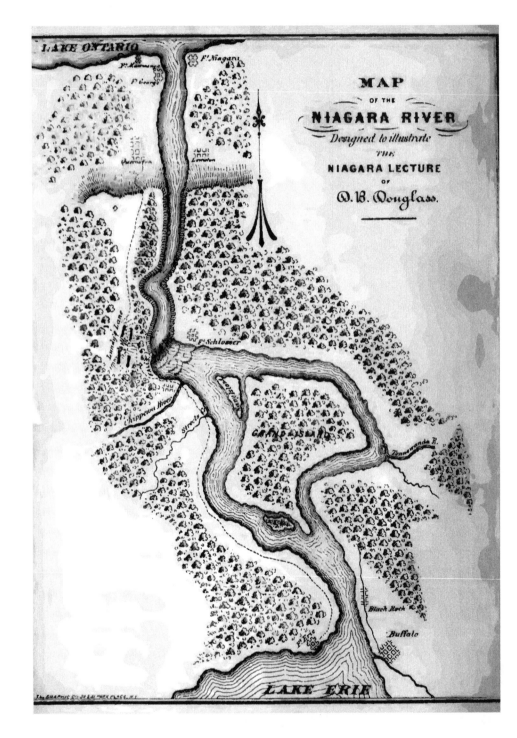

MAP
OF THE
NIAGARA RIVER
Designed to illustrate
THE
NIAGARA LECTURE
OF
D. B. Douglass.

THE
HISTORICAL MAGAZINE.

Vol. II. Third Series.]   JULY, 1873.   [No. 1.

I.—*REMINISCENCES OF THE CAM-*
PAIGN OF 1814, ON THE NIAGA-
RA FRONTIER.

From THE PAPERS OF THE LATE DAVID B. DOUG-
LASS, LL.D., FORMERLY CAPTAIN OF ENGIN-
EERS, U. S. A.; COMMUNICATED BY HIS CHIL-
DREN, FOR PUBLICATION IN THE HISTORICAL
MAGAZINE.

[The author of the following Lectures, Major DAVID B.
DOUGLASS, was a native of Pompton, New Jersey, where
he was born on the twenty-first of March, 1790. He was
graduated at Yale-college, in 1813; entered the Army, as
second-lieutenant of Engineers; and was stationed at
West Point. In the Summer of 1814, he was ordered to
the Niagara frontier, and arrived just in time to take part,
as a volunteer, in the Battle of Niagara. In the subsequent defence of Fort Erie, in August and September, he
distinguished himself, and was, at once, promoted to a
First-lieutenancy, with the brevet rank of Captain.

He was ordered to West Point, on the first of January,
1815, and made Assistant-professor of Natural and Exper-
imental Philosophy.

In 1819, he acted, during the Summer recess, as Astro-
nomical Surveyor of the Boundary Commission, from Niagara to Detroit; and, in the Summer of 1820, he accompanied Governor Cass, in a similar capacity, to the Northwest.
In August, of the same year, while on this duty, he was
promoted to the professorship of Mathematics, in the
Military Academy, at West Point, vacant by the death of
his father-in-law, Professor Andrew Ellicott, with the
rank of Major in the Army. In 1823, he was transferred,
at his own desire, to the Professorship of Civil and Military Engineering.

The science of Engineering was then new, in this country; and few great works had been executed. He devoted himself to it, with unsparing energy, and soon acquired a wide reputation. Many advantageous offers were
made him; but he chose to remain at West Point. He
was, however, employed by the State of Pennsylvania,
during the Summer recesses, from 1826 to 1830, as a Con-
sulting Engineer, and charged with the surveys of several
of the more difficult parts, in its system of public works.
In 1831, he resigned his professorship, and became Chief
Engineer of the Morris Canal, residing in Brooklyn.

In 1833, he was appointed Professor of Civil Architec-
ture, in the new University of the City of New York, and
made the designs for its building, opposite Washing-

In June, 1833, he commenced his surveys for the great
work of supplying the city of New York with water; and,
in November, he submitted his first Report, demonstrat-
ing the feasibility of such a supply, and showing how to
obtain it, from the Croton-river. He reviewed his surveys,
in 1834, and prepared plans and estimates for the city au-
thorities; and, the next Spring, it was determined, by a
vote of the citizens, that the aqueduct should be built.
Water Commissioners were appointed; and Major Douglass was, at once, elected Chief Engineer, and proceeded
to lay out, minutely, the line of the Acqueduct, and to
complete his plans. He had accomplished his preliminary
work when he was superseded.

In 1839, he planned and laid out Greenwood Cemetery,
Brooklyn.

In 1840, he was elected President of Kenyon-college,
Ohio, and removed to Gambier, in the Spring of 1841. He
withdrew from this office, in 1844, and returned to the vicinity of New York.

In 1845-6, he laid out the Cemetery, at Albany; and, in
1847, he was employed in developing the landscape features
of Staten Island. In 1848, he laid out the Protestant Cemetery, at Quebec; and, in the same year, he was elected
Professor of Mathematics and Natural Philosophy, in
Hobart-college, at Geneva, New York. He accepted the
office, and entered upon its duties, in October; and, on the
nineteenth of October, 1849, he died.[*]

These Lectures were prepared with great care and first
delivered, in 1840, before the Mercantile Library Associa-
tion of New York. In the Winter of 1845, after a rigid
revision, they were repeated before the Young Men's As-
sociation, at Albany ; and, afterwards, at the request of
"numerous members of both branches of the Legisla-
"ture," they were again delivered, in the Assembly-
chamber, in the Capitol, in the same city. They were
also delivered at Troy and at New Haven, during the
same Winter. In the early part of 1849, they ere delivered at Buffalo ; and it is believed that they ere read
elsewhere, at different times.

The introductory remarks, preceding the first Lecture,
varied as the audiences varied ; and, sometimes, the local-
ity called out, from the author, some allusion to the past,
either of the place or of some of its inhabitants, preliminary to the Lecture itself. The particular "Introduction"
which has been employed in this publication is that which
was used at New Haven, in the Spring of 1845.

* We are indebted to Appleton's *New American Cyclo-
pedia* for the above sketch of Major Douglass's life and
services.—EDITOR.

It is believed that few papers, concerning the War of 1812, possess greater interest and importance, as material for history, than these Lectures ; and it affords us much pleasure that THE HISTORICAL MAGAZINE has been permitted to present them to its readers, in the first publication of them.—EDITOR.]

LECTURE FIRST.

At the request of the Managers of the Young Men's Institute, I am to give you, in this and the following Lectures, some account of the military scenes and events of the Campaign of 1814, on the Niagara.

And, in recurring to these reminiscences of my early professional life, I must be permitted, in the outset, to express the deep emotion with which I find myself in the presence of a New Haven audience; for it was here, in this city, in the midst of associations which I dearly love to cherish, that I first conceived the idea of becoming a professional soldier, and received a large portion of the impressions which, whether in that profession or out of it, have given a character and coloring to my whole subsequent life.

It was in the Summer of 1813, during the pendency of the War—those will remember, whose recollections go back to that period. Large armies, drawn from the population of different districts of our country, were in the field; nearly the whole of our immense frontier was the theatre of actual War; the mails were loaded down and the press teemed with the stirring events of both pleasing and painful interest passing around us. A very high degree of military feeling pervaded the whole country. Even this city, threatened with attack from the British Squadron blockading New London and, sometimes, making its appearance further down the Sound, had its *elite* organized for instant service; and the streets wore an appearance not unlike that of a frontier town. It is not surprising that, under such influences, and with a mind naturally predisposed to military enterprise, I should have adopted *that* as the profession of my life.

With an education much superior to that of most aspirants of that period, I aspired, of course, to the higher department of the service —the Corps of Engineers; and my application was so favored, by this circumstance, that, thirty days after I received my degree from President Dwight, in the Church across the Green, I was a Second-lieutenant of that Corps. Nearly all the events then of which I am to speak, happened within a short year from the termination of my College-life; and, amidst the strange vicissitudes of that eventful year, how often did my thoughts revert back to the quiet retreats of Yale-college, scarcely able, in so great a change of scene, to realize my own personal identity.

The human race, it has been philosophically remarked, may be regarded, in a certain sense, collectively, as an individual man; having had its infancy, in the early ages of the world; its progress from youth to manhood, marked by the gradual development of its intellectual and moral powers, in after times; and its full maturity consummated, or yet to be consummated, at some later period. Whether the race is destined still to go on, progressively, to some ulterior state of advancement, or, like its parallel, in human life, to sink, back again, through the phases of a descending scale, to a second childhood; and whether, in the latter case, it has, or has not, yet passed its grand climacteric, are questions which time only can solve. The analogy might not hold good, in every particular, and yet be true and instructive, as undoubtedly it is, in the main.

But there is another and more obvious application of the same idea, not to the race, collectively, but to the particular States and Nations into which it has been distributed. This is a most natural thought. The mind, of its own accord, and almost without any external suggestion, invests Nations with the attributes of individual and personal character. We trace the time and circumstances of their birth; we follow them, in their growth and progress, from the weakness and imbecility of infancy, to the strength and vigor of mature age; we contemplate their gradual improvement in knowledge, refinement, letters, and the liberal arts; we discriminate among them, as among individuals, diversities of character; and we are not slow in detecting those particularities of circumstance and condition which may have operated in producing those diversities. Finally, we follow those that have passed it, through the period of their greatest development; and, finally, too, through the successive stages of the inverted series of their decline and fall; and only turn from the contemplation, at last, when, as in the case of individuals, passed from the stage of life, the places which once knew them know them no more.

Regarding, in this aspect, the individuality of the social and political state, it follows, naturally—and history abundantly sustains it, as part of the constitution of things in which we live —that nations, like individuals, are here in a disciplinary state. In the earlier periods of their existence, they are, as it were, in the hands, and sometimes under the rod, of the schoolmaster, receiving, in some sense, for good or for evil, an education; having before them opportunities, to be improved or neglected, for the culture of the powers and susceptibilities of the common mind; for the cultivation of right moral impulses—right practical habits; and, in short, for the formation of a moral and intellectual character, suited to the responsibilities and dignity of after life. Even at mature age, instruction is not discontinued. The whole of the life of an individual man is but an education; and a Nation, with its own experience and the experience of other nations to guide, instruct, reprove, and warn, can never be without something to learn. Nor can such lessons be neglected, nor such opportunities abused, with impunity, any more by nations than by individuals. The retributions of the former are, indeed, temporal, but not, therefore, the less certain.

The interest of these remarks, on the present occasion, arises from their application to our own particular circumstances, as a nation. In the scale of history, we have passed but a very brief period since the beginning of our political existence—not more than sufficient, ordinarily, to have brought us across the threshold of our pupilage—and yet we are already filling no inconsiderable place in the community of nations. This rapid acquisition of power, station, and influence suggests a peculiar necessity for our looking well to our ways, and treasuring up, only the more carefully, the fruits of our past experience, for our guidance in future. And yet it is to be feared that, like other children of prosperity, we are more inclined to exult in the brilliancy of our success than to draw a moral lesson from it—like them, too apt, in the ardor of our pursuit of what is present and future, to forget what is past. A single fact in connection with the subject matter of which I am to speak, will illustrate the truth of this remark.

A few years since, I was requested by an institution, in the city of New York, to throw together, in the form of a Lecture, my personal reminiscences of the Niagara Campaign. As I was very young, at the epoch of that Campaign, I naturally looked around, with a view to meet this request, for such documents and memoirs as, it was reasonable to believe, had been published on the subject; and, to my amazement, I found none—except the brief and hasty despatches of the different commanders, written at the moment, there was nothing. Not only the Niagara Campaign, but the whole War—I speak of its *military* events—was already passed, or rapidly passing, into oblivion, even to those who had been personally concerned with it. To myself, the events of the Niagara Campaign were, generally, very familiar; but, having derived my knowledge of them from my participation in them and my personal intercourse with my brother officers, I was not,

until I made the inquiry, aware how very great was the deficiency of historic records to the world at large.

Surely there was something wrong here: there must have been some defect, either of national feeling or of historic interest, to account for such a deficiency. The War was not a small one. It was fought against one of the most powerful nations on the globe; it occupied three Campaigns; it called forth the active energies of the whole country; and led to the organization of our whole inland and maritime frontier. Military operations of great scope and compass were embraced in it; many desperate battles fought—sometimes attended with defeat, it is true, but not the less valuable and instructive, as matter of experience, on that account; while, on the other hand, there was no inconsiderable number of contests well sustained, and some fairly to be claimed as victories gained.

There was surely no lack of interest in the subject; and yet, after an interval of thirty years, no historian had been found to record these events, either for the honor of the country or its guidance in a future War. Even the Regiments which fought on our side had been dismembered, broken up, and scattered, and the record of their respective achievements utterly lost; while those that fought against us had been enriched with every species of armorial honor; and, even to this hour, in every part of the world where they appear, to be quartered, they are paraded under the historic memorials of our NIAGARA, our FORT ERIE, our PLATTSBURG, and our BALTIMORE, in common with those of VITTORIA, SALAMANCA, and the PYRENEES.

There are some, perhaps, who find an excuse for the indifference, to which I have alluded, in the errors and disasters of the War, as if the national pride might be wounded by an impartial narrative. Such a sentiment has, not unfrequently, been expressed in my hearing; but can it be needful to repel it, on this occasion and before this audience? If it were well-founded, how weak would it be to shut our eyes to the lessons of experience from any consideration of this kind. In the discipline of common life, our most useful lessons are often drawn from our most painful experiences; and, in the complicated operations of War, neither the *esprit de corps* nor the higher tactics are to be acquired without severe conflicts and some humiliating trials of disaster and defeat. If the fact were, indeed, as the objectors represent, it would be the *more* necessary for us to make it matter of history, that we might be guarded against the like disasters, in future—for history is the memory of the State.

But the fact is not so: the early Campaigns of the War were, undoubtedly, disastrous; but could it have been expected otherwise? A Peace, scarcely interrupted for thirty years, had, in a great measure, neutralized the experience acquired in the War of the Revolution; so that we had not only soldiers to raise and train, and stores to provide, but Staff departments, of all kinds, to create; arsenals and depots to organize; frontiers to entrench and fortify; and, above all, to acquire that systematic unity of action, which is indispensable to the success of military operations of the State. These things are the work of much time. A resolve of Congress may call into service a hundred thousand men; and a very short time would suffice, with good drill-masters, to give them elementary discipline. But of what avail would it all be, without the higher discipline and the mature experience necessary to provide for all their multifarious wants and to direct, and move, and marshal, and use them with advantage, at the precise point of time and place, on so vast a field of action as ours? I confess, when I look at the great superiority of our late enemy, in all these respects—his long experience; his habitual and perfect organization; his veteran Battalions, disciplined in the War of the Peninsula, and coming hither, flushed with victory—I am rather astonished that the War was not tenfold more disastrous than it was. Captious criticism may doubtless find errors enough, and the critic may employ himself, if he choose, in magnifying and distorting them; but I defy him to make a case of national dishonor, even if it were admitted that the first two Campaigns were disastrous, when the third found us front to front with those very Battalions, coping with them, with crossed bayonets, in such a strife as that of Lundy's-lane.

The history of the War, if written at all, must be written soon, as the time of collecting materials is rapidly passing away. The substantial matter must be drawn chiefly from personal sources; and these, I am grieved to say, are every day becoming fewer and fewer. Even now, I look round me, in vain, for the groups of gallant men with whom it was my privilege to be associated, in the Niagara Army. Of the Engineer Corps of that Army, I am the only survivor; and of the chosen circle, to the number of twenty, from various Corps—kindred spirits, who used, nightly, to assemble at the Engineer mess-room, at Fort Erie—only two or three remain. To my mind's eye, indeed, I find it not difficult to recall, at pleasure, the living, breathing forms and lineaments of my old comrades and friends; but, to my corporal sense, they are gone.*

* In the manuscript, at this place, there is a line of as-

Before speaking of the events of the Niagar Campaign, in particular, I must request of you moment's attention to some of its external rela tions; the military attitude of the frontier, the time it was fought; and the particular trai of events which led to its organization.

The political circumstances under which th War was declared involved, as a sort of mora necessity, an imperfect state of preparation, o our part. Whatever may have been the pre ponderance of public opinion, in its favor there was, in the differences of political sent ment or in the antagonisms of party, at th time, enough of opposition to defeat any forma measures, in anticipation of it, so long as th chances of its occurrence were only contingen Even after it became, in the eye of the sag acious and far-reaching statesman, inevitable the country was slow to realize its approach slow, even then, to make any prudent prepara tion for it; nor did they so, in fact, till the que tion was irretrievably settled by the actual de claration of War. The Rubicon once passed and all possibility of retreat thus excluded, the for the first time, seriously and in good earnes we began the work of preparation.

Our enemy, however, in the mean time, wa by no means, thus dilatory. Greatly our super ior, then, at least, in the personal organizatio and discipline of his forces; more accustome to the active enterprises of war; and, habitually more prompt and decisive in all his militar movements; he was enabled, while his number were yet inconsiderable, to anticipate us, no only in the points of attack, but in the time an mode of the assault. A character was thus giv en, at the outset, to the military policy of th first two Campaigns. Instead of being activ and aggressive, as they were intended to hav been, they became eminently *defensive;* and for a long time, even as late as the middle o the second Campaign, the energies of the coun try, which should have been directed to a regu lar systematic invasion of Canada, were almo wholly absorbed in measures for repelling pett partisan attacks.

On the remote North-western frontier, ou exposure to this species of warfare was particu

terisks, which indicates the fact that, on the subject las referred to, in the text, Major Douglass was in the habi while lecturing, of extemporizing further than he wrote.

It is to be regretted, since they are now matter of his tory, that the portraits of those who were thus assembled in commands of greater or less importance, on the Niag ara frontier, in 1814, as those portraits were thus presen ed by so capable a hand, have not been preserved for th benefit of those, coming after, who shall incline to th study of the history of that yet unfashionable subject.— Editor.

larly great. The vast border country, on that quarter, was inhabited by numerous and powerful tribes of Indians, through whose territory the jurisdictional limits of the two powers had never been defined, and whose allegiance, in point of fact, had been secured, by a long course of protection and friendly policy, exclusively to the British Government. To overawe these Indians, probably more than to operate extensively upon Canada, at that remote point, the expedition of General Hull had been put in motion, even before the declaration of War; and, having a considerable force of Militia, concentrated at Detroit, soon after that event, it crossed the river and commenced an invasion of Upper Canada, at that point.

The theory of this movement was, undoubtedly, correct; and if its legitimate object had been reached by a reasonable amount of enterprise and skill, in its execution, it would have ensured safety and peace to the scattered frontier settlements, for whose protection it was designed, and put an end to the War, in that quarter. But, unfortunately, in this respect, it was a failure. It retired, timidly, before the first demonstration of hostile force; and the disgraceful capitulation of Detroit, which followed, soon after, placed those settlements in a far worse position than they would have been, if this movement had not been attempted.

The enemy, by this and other advantages obtained, in the same neighborhood, immediately acquired possession of the whole Indian territory, including our own peninsula of Michigan, and, with it, a more unlimited control than ever over its savage population; while we, on our part, were not only thrown upon the defensive, but obliged to marshal our line of defence far within our own territory.

The organization of that defence, on the remote frontier of Ohio, under circumstances of peculiar difficulty and discouragement, is one of the brightest passages in the history of the War. In the depth of an inclement Winter, at a distance from any settlement capable of affording aid or supplies, in the presence of an enterprising enemy, crowned with success, hitherto, and daily increasing in force and self-confidence, by the most extraordinary efforts, forts and intrenchments were built; roads opened; troops levied, and brought from remote places into line; and supplies of arms, munitions, and stores collected and transported, hundreds of miles, on pack horses, through the wilderness. All this done, and, in the short space of two months, such an attitude of defence attained, that the most desperate and determined assaults of the hitherto victorious enemy were wholly [un]able to make any effective impression upon it. The tide of War, in that quarter, was thus,

at length, turned; and, towards the Summer of the second Campaign, the British Commander, having been foiled, with great loss, in all his attempts upon the positions of his adversary, abandoned further operations, and fell back to Malden and De'roit, to wait the event of the approaching contest on the lake.

On the tenth of September, 1813, was fought the memorable naval-battle of Lake Erie, in which, in the chaste and beautiful language of Commodore Perry's despatch, "It pleased the "Almighty to give to the arms of the United "States, a signal victory over their enemies on "that lake." This event, besides giving us the naval ascendency on Lake Erie, changed, entirely, the relative situation of the contending parties, on the land. General Harrison, having now no apprehension of danger to his right flank, assumed the offensive and compelled his antagonist, in turn, to retreat. The recapture of Detroit and the capture of the Canadian posts, on the opposite side of the river, was a thing of course; and the complete overthrow of the hostile Army, in the battle of the Moravian towns, in Upper Canada, on the fifth of October, following, restored the Indian tribes to their rightful jurisdiction, and gave a triumphant termination to the Campaign and all further hostilities, on that frontier.

Looking, now, at the corresponding operations, on the lower part of the frontier, we notice, that, while the War of nearly two Campaigns had been thus brought to a successful close, in the Nor'hwest, down to the date of its final and decisive battle in October, no strategical movement, in the proper sense, had taken place on any other part ot the line. Troops and levies were collected in considerable numbers, particularly on the Niagara border, in 1812; and, in the latter part of that year, several attempts were made to gain a footing, on the Canada side of the Strait. The assault upon Queenston Heights stands conspicuous among these, as an example of determined bravery, on the part of those engaged in it; but, like all other attempts of the like kind, it was ultimately unsuccessful; and the Campaign closed without any advantage really gained in the prosecution of the War, and without any movement of a more general character.

The commencement of the year 1813, found a naval armament organized on Lake Ontario, and a large land force, of different arms, collected at Sackett's-harbor; and, in the month of April, of that year, a combined expedition of land and naval force was fitted out and directed against the post and depot of Little York, the seat of government of Upper Canada. The capture of this post was effected in the face of a strong force, though not without severe loss;

and, the works and stores being destroyed, the expedition united with the troops at Fort Niagara, and, with them, made a forcible descent upon the peninsula of Upper Canada, at that point. The British forts were captured, on the twenty-seventh of May, and a large American force took possession of the country, in advance of Fort George; but, as the opposing Army was strongly reinforced, about the same time, they failed of accomplishing any ulterior aim, and merely occupied their intrenched camp, at Fort George, through the Summer.

This expedition, from its imposing character, in point of force, the range of its operations, and the success of its *first* enterprises, may be considered an interesting episode to the Campaign of 1813, and, doubtless, had some influence, at first, upon the tone of public opinion; but, as it seems to have had no manifest reference to the systematic prosecution of the War, and really made no essential change in the relation of the belligerent parties, I have not considered it an exception to the remark, heretofore made, although it occurred before the termination of General Harrison's Campaign. In the eye of strict military criticism, it must be regarded as a desultory operation, however distinguished it may have been, in examples of courage, discipline, and personal achievement.

Of a very different character, however, in its design, as well as in the force organized for its accomplishment, was the expedition set on foot, towards the close of this Campaign, for the invasion of Lower Canada and the capture of Montreal. According to the project of that expedition, two Armies, taking their departures, respectively, from Sackett's-harbor and Plattsburg—one near the outlet of Lake Ontario, and the other at the nearest adjacent point of Lake Champlain—were to advance to a common point, on the St. Lawrence, at some distance above Montreal, and, there, unite, and proceed, with great force and promptness, to the ultimate object of the expedition—the occupation of Montreal.

The command-in-chief, on the Canada frontier, had recently been assigned to General Wilkinson, whose long experience in service was thought to give him a claim to this distinction; and, by him, the organization and movement, at Sackett's-harbor, was personally superintended; while to General Hampton, another officer of the old Army, were assigned the corresponding arrangements of the Plattsburg Divison.

Towards the latter part of the month of October, the Sackett's-harbor column, strengthened by the junction of the Niagara Army and the disposable force, from all the intervening posts,

to the number of about seven thousand men, was organized and equipped with means of transport, for the descent of the St. Lawrence; and, on the twenty-fifth of that month, it was accordingly put in motion. The descent of the river, although opposed, of course, by every means which the enemy could bring to bear upon it, appears to have been well ordered and, for the most part, skillfully managed; and, although the flanking parties and guards were frequently engaged in skirmishes requiring strong reinforcements—in one instance amounting to a pitched battle—the main body of the Army succeeded, without serious loss, in passing all the garrisons and strong places of the route; and, on the eleventh of November, reached a point, near St. Regis, at which the co-operation of the right column was expected to commence.

The movements of that column, in the mean time, having converged to within seventy or eighty miles of the point of junction, had been suddenly suspended by its General, on the ground that the aggregate of stores and supplies, in the two Armies, would not be sufficient for the subsistence of the whole, in the meditated enterprise; and, without awaiting further orders, after stating this opinion, the column was immediately put upon a retrograde march, and conducted back to Plattsburg. The Commander-in-chief being thus deprived of the expected co-operation, after counseling with his officers, abandoned the attack upon Montreal, and retired into Winter-quarters, at French Mills; and the expedition, upon which so much labor and means had been expended, and from which a decisive result had been so confidently expected, was thus terminated, by causes within ourselves, in utter failure and defeat.

It would not be consistent with the object of this brief outline, to assign the responsibilities or to analyze the delinquency of the parties in this extraordinary failure. It would be impossible, however, for any well-regulated mind to contemplate, without repugnance, the breach of military subordination, if not the culpable negligence, connected with it; nor is it very easy to account for their occurrence, except with a knowledge of the fact—which ought, doubtless, to have been previously considered—that the two Generals were on terms of bitter personal hostility with each other.

It would be difficult for any one, whose personal recollections do not go back to the period of which I am speaking, to realize the feeling of disappointment and regret which came over the country, by reason of this failure.

Two seasons of the War had transpired, not inactively, but without any direct tangible result tending towards its termination; the public mind, naturally becoming impatient and dissatisfied under these circumstances, had caught, with avidity, the first development of the present enterprise, and watched it with no common interest, as it advanced. In proportion as it seemed to approach its object, expectation became more and more intense; and when, at last, in direct opposition to the popular assurance of its success, the news of its failure arrived, and when it was found that the elements of this failure were among ourselves, the state of public feeling can better be conceived than described. Investigations and Courts Martial were, of course, instituted, and a long series of recriminations, fruitful in nothing but bad feeling and personality, ensued; but, as they are irrelevant to the present occasion, we pass them without further notice. The public mind, indeed, had scarcely time to dwell upon them, before it was diverted to a new train of events, on the Niagara frontier.

The military occupation of that frontier, in the early part of the Campaign, had naturally led to the formation of a strong opposing Corps, on the part of the enemy; and a portion of that Corps remained, after our troops, except garrisons in the forts, had been withdrawn. These garrisons were composed chiefly of levies and volunteers, engaged for various and uncertain periods; and not being always regularly replaced, as their times expired, the aggregate strength gradually diminished, until it became necessary, at last, to abandon the forts on the British side. In doing this, the commanding officer, under a mistaken apprehension of his orders, set fire to and destroyed the neighboring village of Newark; and, in this inconsiderate and unjustifiable act, as it gave a pretext for a barbarous and inhuman retaliation, originated, as we shall see, the Niagara Campaign and, to a very considerable extent, the subsequent policy of the whole Canada War.

The act was promptly disavowed by the superior authority, and by the Government; but the disclaimer seems to have had no effect in allaying the feeling of hostility which had been kindled; and, unfortunately, the occasion of retaliation was not long in presenting itself. The evacuation of Fort George took place on the tenth of December, Fort Niagara being left, with a moderate garrison, at the same time, without any apprehension of immediate danger. On the nineteenth of the month, however, a strong detachment of the enemy, under cover of night, and presuming, doubtless, upon the assurance of security, on our part, crossed the river, near Lewiston; approached the fort, without opposition; and took it, by surprise, after a short conflict. Large bodies of Indians and Volunteers crossed, immediately after, and commenced, at Lewiston and Youngstown, the work of devastation; and, before the end of the month, the whole line of the frontier, from Lake Ontario to Lake Erie, was, in the hands of these marauders, a scene of indiscriminate conflagration and cruelty.

Such was the melancholy termination of the eventful and varied year of 1813. And, having followed the main line of its military policy, without regard to incidental events, I shall recapitulate the condition in which it left the different portions of the frontier, as follows: The North-western wilderness, with its Indian hordes subdued and held firmly in check by the decisive victories of General Harrison and the triumph on Lake Erie: the North-eastern border, nearly as at the beginning of the Campaign, except a much larger force in the field, a higher state of discipline and *esprit de corps*, and some experience in the more difficult sciences of military administration and the tactics of Campaigns: between these extremes, the Niagara frontier had been snatched, momentarily, from us and desolated with fire and sword.

With these preliminaries, we may now approach the Campaign of 1814, prepared to appreciate the circumstances under which the Niagara portion of it was planned, organized, and executed. The cruel barbarity which had been introduced, on that frontier—repugnant to common humanity, as to the laws and usages of all civilized warfare—the individual injury sustained, in person and property, by thousands of unoffending and peaceful citizens; and the general feeling of insecurity and alarm, created along the whole New York frontier, rendered it imperative upon the Government that some measure of reparation should be adopted, without delay—not, indeed, to retaliate outrage with outrage; but, on the contrary, to put an end to this miserable strife; to re-assert the rights of humanity, in the conduct of the War; and to give to the peaceful citizen some assurance of domestic safety and protection. Thus much was required in the cause of humanity; but there were other considerations also to be regarded, in the organization of that Campaign. It was of no small consequence, in a military sense, to re-occupy the captured posts, particularly Fort Niagara, at all hazards. The attempt to do this would, of course, operate as a *diversion* in drawing the troops of the enemy from his positions, below; and, when the time for taking advantage of that diversion should come, experience had shown how easy it would be, by a proper concert of action between the land and naval forces—we having possession of the lake—to snatch away the Division thus employed, on the Niagara frontier, and use it in a combined attack upon Kingston and Prescott. And this was the theory of the Niagara Campaign: Firstly, to re-occupy that frontier, in force; Secondly, to divert the enemy from his lower posts; and, Thirdly, to be in a position, if necessary, to take advantage of that diversion, whenever the time should arrive or the occasion offer for so doing.

The first suggestion of these considerations appears to have come, on the spur of the occasion, from the Executive of New York. Addressing the Secretary of War, on the second of January, immediately after the news of the Niagara outrages reached him, and in anticipation of others, of the same kind, Governor Tompkins thus wrote: "To counteract these Winter ex- "peditions of the enemy, it will be indispensa- "ble that our Army be in motion. I would "throw out for consideration, whether the whole "force at French Mills and Plattsburg ought not "to be removed to Ogdensburg or Sackett's har- "bor, and, acting in concert with the force at "the latter place, attack Prescott or Kingston; "or whether, if *that* be deemed impracticable, "twenty five hundred of the Army cannot be "conveyed to the Niagara frontier, and, with "the Militia and Volunteers—I pledge myself "there shall be five thousand Volunteers, pro- "vided the above number of Regulars be as- "sociated with them—make a diversion from "Kingston and Presrott, whilst the residue of "the Army, with Commodore Chauncey's force, "assails one of those places."

The last of these suggestions was adopted, and began immediately to be acted upon, by the Secretary of War. General Scott, then a Colonel, but, soon after, promoted to a Brigadier, was first put under orders, and, within thirty days after the burning of Buffalo, had already commenced the formation of a Corps for that frontier. General Brown was simultaneously detached from French Mills, with a force of two thousand Infantry and a proportionate Corps of Artillery, to reach Sackett's-harbor, by a forced march, in the depth of Winter, and, afterwards, to proceed also to the same scene of action. Other officers of distinguished merit and gallantry were understood to be detailed for that service; and the report soon became current, in the circles of the Army, that a strong corps of picked troops was to be formed, on this frontier, under the command of Major-general Brown, seconded by General Scott and others of the same stamp, to be employed in the recapture of the forts, and such other active enterprises as the fortune of War might place within its reach.

The expectation that the capture of Fort Niagara would require the operations of a regular siege, bringing into use the arm of Engineering, in its most important and responsible character —an opportunity seldom enjoyed in our service— created no little interest among the officers of Engineers to whom it became known; and, when it was further rumored that two of the most eminent and distinguished members of that Corps—Major, afterwards Colonel, McRee, and Brevet Major Wood—were to be included in the detail, for this high duty, the desire to participate in it, so far as the circumstances became known, was intense.

During the pendency of these interesting movements, in the latter part of the month of January and the beginning of February, it was *my* peculiar good fortune to enjoy the society and friendship of the last-mentioned officer, at West Point, he having just returned, with great eclat, from the scenes of the North-western Campaign; and I, a junior Subaltern of Engineers, preparing myself, by study and military exercises, for active duties to come.

West Point was not, then, as it now is, during the Winter, a place of studious enterprise and zeal to an organized Corps of Cadets. The Corps, authorized by the law of 1812, had not yet come into being; and to the few Cadets, previously attached, the Winter was a season of relaxation; and most of them were absent, in vacation, at the time here referred to.

The chief importance of the post arose from its being the rendezvous and, generally, the head-quarters of the Corps of Engineers; and there was a garrison of soldiers, enlisted expressly for that branch of service, called the Company of "Bombardiers, Sappers, and Miners," the command of which, for the time being, had been assigned to me.

The obvious relation between the duty and discipline of this Company and the chief anticipated enterprise of the Niagara Campaign naturally suggested its designation as an appendage to that Army. At all events, it was permitted me to enjoy the assurance that I should be included in the detail for that Corps; and, from that time forth, until the departure of my gallant friend, it was our custom to occupy the disposable part of every day, and often whole nights, in analyzing the events of the preceding Campaign or in developing, with as much minuteness as the case admitted, the anticipated plans and operations of that to come.

I am somewhat particular, in making these statements, to repel an assertion which has found a place in some of the memoirs of that period; viz.: that the Order, given in March, to General Brown, to proceed to and operate upon the Niagara frontier, was intended and indicated as a *feint*, but, being misunderstood, in that sense, by the General, the Campaign, with all its hard-fought battles, was entirely the result of this paltry mistake.

I do not pretend to know what may have transpired between General Brown and the Secretary of War—it is but hypothetically set forth, in the statement referred to—but it does not appear, even from that statement, that he transcended the discretion committed to him; and that there was no great mistake—on the contrary, that he acted in conformity with a settled plan—I am constrained, implicitly, to believe from the evidence already in part adduced. As early as the first of February, before General Brown could have left French Mills, it was known, at West Point, through the correspondence of Major Wood, the substance of which was communicated to me, at the time, not only that such a Campaign as I have described was to be organised, but that General Brown was to be its commander. The selection was a very natural and proper one. General Brown had commanded the elite of the Army—the special Corps selected for its protection in the descent of the St. Lawrence, the preceding Autumn—had gained a character in the discharge of that duty; was altogether a popular General : at all events, the fact of his being selected must have been settled, somewhere, to have been spoken of, as it was, at that time; and it is not easy to perceive, in consistency with this conclusion, how the Campaign could, in any respect, have been the result of a misapprehension of orders, in the month of March following. But I return to my narrative.

On the twelfth of February, my friend, Colonel Wood, left West Point, and repaired, first to Albany and then to Canandaigua, to take part in the preparatory arrangements for the Campaign. On the twenty-first, in a letter written, at the moment of his departure from Albany, he alluded to the subject, in the following terms : "A train of field-artillery has already left this, "for the Niagara frontier, and it is expected "that a Battery train will immediately follow, "for the same destination ; so you can form your "own opinion as to the nature and extent of the "meditated operations. It is now, more than "ever, probable that your services, as an Engin- "eer in the field, will soon be required. Gov- "ernor Tompkins tells me that a large force of "Militia is already collected at Eleven Mile- "creek ; and that other troops are soon to join "the Army, near Buffalo. I hope we shall be "able to do something for the honor of the ser- "vice, in the spring."

From the date of this letter, as the Spring advanced, troops, of all descriptions, for the new Army Corps, were in rapid motion towards the scene of its contemplated action; and Buffalo, or rather the site where Buffalo had been, being the place of rendezvous, soon put off its aspect of desolation, and became an animated scene of the most active and busy preparation. The Reg-

ular troops, as they arrived, were organized into two Brigades, under Generals Scott and Ripley. The Militia and Volunteers of New York and Pennsylvania, under General Porter, formed another Brigade. A fine Battalion of Artillery and battery-train, placed under the command of Major Hindman, with a detachment of Cavalry, under Captain Harris, completed the the active force. To these were added a Corps of Engineers, and the various departments—Adjutant's, Quarter master's, Inspector's, Commissary's, and Medical—of a General Staff ;—and the whole, as it began to assume an air of organization, was designated the Second Division, or left wing, of the Northern Army. In the mean time, stores, munitions, and equipments were also collected ; vehicles and other transports provided ; and all the means and appliances of an active and vigorous Campaign gradually, but steadily, tended to their completion.

Long before they were completed, in fact, however, the troops, as they came in, had been formed into a Camp of Instruction, and put upon a rigorous system of drills and field-exercises, calculated to develope, at the eve of its requirement, the full extent of their powers as a fighting Corps. Since the days of the Revolution, our country had probably never seen a more thorough and efficient drill than that here spoken of ; nor have the immediate benefits of such discipline been often more conspicuously manifest. Even the Militia levies, under the influence of its example, participated eminently in its good effects, and showed, on various occasions, during the Campaign, a coolness and intrepidity worthy of veteran soldiers.

The difference, I may remark, in passing, between soldiers and Militia—I use the term in no individual sense—does not consist, as many are apt to imagine, in the better acquaintance of the former with the movements and evolutions of War; nor yet in their greater familiarity with danger—still less in a higher degree of personal courage, for, in this respect, the advantage may be, and often is, on the side of the Militia-man—but in *this*, that the Militia-man, however courageous he may be, individually, has not learned to depend upon the courage and firmness of those around him. He has no practical experience that A. B. and C., on his right and left, will not run off and leave him alone, the moment any very imminent danger threatens ; and, although, perhaps, not very easily alarmed, when he measures the immense disparity of force between the enemy's column and himself, alone, he, at once and very naturally, decides that *discretion is the better part of valor*.

The disciplined soldier, on the other hand, has been trained and drilled, shoulder to shoulder, with his fellows ; and he has merged his individuality--incorporated himself, as it were--in the Corps of which he is a member. For himself, in particular, when danger impends, he has, comparatively no consideration : it is his Regiment, not himself, that is to cope with it; and he feels that the firm sinews and stout hearts around him, blended, as it were, into one personality and animated by one spirit, are not to be moved by a sense of danger.

The effect of discipline then, is to unite and combine the elements of strength into a mass ; and the relative firmness of an undisciplined and disciplined soldiery may be likened to that of a vast number of threads or fibres which, when loose and unequally strained, are broken, one by one, with the slightest weight; but, when twisted into a firm compact cable, may almost defy the utmost stretch of human power to sever it.

It was a kind Providence that put it into the hearts of our Generals, thus to train and discipline that Army, in anticipation of the approaching contest; for if we regard, now, the note of preparation, on the other side, we shall find a force converging to the same frontier, which will presently put their discipline and firmness to the test.

You remember that, previous to the year 1814, Great Britain had sustained the War in Canada simultaneously with her vast military operations on the Continent of Europe ; but that the pacification of Europe, in the early part of that year, putting an end to those operations, enabled her to withdraw a portion of the force, thus employed, and direct it against us.

Early in the month of May, the advance of these reinforcements, having been embarked directly from Bordeaux, began to arrive in Canada ; and, by the opening of the Niagara Campaign, several Regiments of these and other veteran troops, relieved from duty in the lower Provinces, were in rapid movement towards the frontier. The possession of Fort Niagara, the successful incursion of the preceding Winter, and the consequent depopulation of that border, naturally suggested it as a vulnerable point, proper for the commencement of a more formidable invasion ; and such would, undoubtedly, have been the policy of the enemy, had the frontier been found unoccupied in force, or less obstinately contested than it was.

Such are the reflections suggested by the state of things, in the early part of the month of June. The opening of the Campaign was then daily expected; and, in the retirement of West Point—not yet having received my orders—I began to fear that my anticipations of service, in that quarter, were not to be realized. At length, however, after a long and tedious interval, on the sixteenth of that month, they came to hand ;

and I was directed to proceed, forthwith, with the Company under my command, and join the North-western Army, under Major-general Brown.

The Company was taken entirely by surprise. The intended movement had been carefully concealed from them, lest some traverse interest should be made to prevent the issuing of the Order. It did operate rather hardly upon them. They had been recruited under an impression, totally unauthorized, that they would remain, permanently, at West Point ; some of them, it turned out, had even enlisted to avoid Militia draft for the lines; more than half of them were married; and all quietly barracked, at the Point, as they supposed, for the year to come, at least. The Order came among them with the suddenness of a supernatural visitation. But it is due to them to say, that they behaved well, on the occasion. They were, in reality, as fine a set of men as the service could boast; and when recovered from their first surprise, united, with hearty good will, in the arrangements for their departure. Within fifteen minutes after the publication of the Order, I had their knapsacks spread out on Parade, for inspection ; and, in little more than an hour, they were drawn up, at .the public store, to receive their extra supplies. The Order was published at the drumhead, on the sixteenth, at eleven o'clock ; and, on the nineteenth, at evening, all our adieus had been made, and we embarked, under a parting salute, for Albany.*

A slow sailing-craft passage, up the river, delayed us until the twenty-fifth, in leaving Albany ; but, after that, our progress, no longer retarded by adverse winds or tides, was steadily forward ; and, although the weather was intensely hot and sometimes rainy, we accomplished the march of three hundred and sixty miles, in thirteen marching days. At Canandaigua, on the fifth of July, we met the interesting intelligence that the Army had crossed the strait, on the morning of the third, at day-break ; and that Fort Erie had capitulated, with only a slight resistance, immediately after. This report, of course, added new speed to our motion; and every person we met on the road was interrogated, without ceremony, for news. Nothing further of consequence however was obtained, until the morning of the seventh, when the confused rumor of a battle fought, first met us, at Genesee-river. In the course of the day, as we advanced, it became certain that an important

* "At the eve of our departure, I had the happiness to be allowed the companionship of Lieutenant Story, recently appointed in the Corps of Engineers, who had obtained orders attaching him to the Company, and took the field with us."—*Major Douglass.*

battle had, in fact, been fought on the plains of Chippewa, with a decided advantage, it was said, on our side; and that the Army was already in motion, in pursuit.

We were now rapidly approaching the scene of many and long cherished anticipations. Another day was to bring us within the sound of the artillery; and the occurrence of these rumors, as we approached—at first, vague; then, more determinate; and, at last, clear and definite on matters of the greatest moment—gave increasing interest, at every step of our progress.

On the ninth of July, at noon, we arrived at Buffalo—not the enterprising, busy metropolis of Western New York, as it now is, spreading its noble avenues, miles in length, on every side, and rearing aloft its stately edifices and glittering domes; but a wide, desolate expanse, with only two small houses visible; a few rude sheds and shanties; a soiled tent, here and there; and, in one or two places, a row of marquees, of a better sort, apparently giving shelter to some wounded men. These were all the habitations, or substitutes for habitations, the place afforded. Half a dozen isolated sentinels were seen on post, keeping guard over as many irregular piles of loose stores and camp-equipage; and the ground, recently occupied by the camp—thick set with rows of measured squares, worn smooth on the surface, and scattered, here and there, with fragments of soldiers' clothes, old belts, and accoutrements, of various kinds—gave an air of desolation to the whole scene, only rendered the more striking by these details; and, in fact, Buffalo, just deserted by the busy groups which had, a few days before, occupied it, was desert and comfortless, beyond any power of mine to describe. The two buildings were, above and below, filled with wounded officers from the Battle of Chippewa; and here, during an hour's halt, under no very pleasing auspices, commenced our intercourse with the realities of War.

We had little time to linger, however. The goal of our present aim was still in advance. The Army was understood to be at Chippewa, eighteen miles down the river; and this further distance was to be accomplished, if possible, before the Company had rest. Here, however, a difficulty occurred, as to the means of transport—every vehicle was in Canada; and our wagoners, having been engaged only to Buffalo, refused to cross the river. Persuasions, promises, and threats were exhausted upon them, in vain; and there seemed no alternative but to pitch our camp at Buffalo, for the night. At this stage of our embarrassment, however, it was recollected, fortunately, that a launch, or hulk, of eighteen or twenty tons burden, was laying at Black Rock, two miles below; and thither we according'y marched, without a moment's delay.

The launch was on shore, at high-water mark, and badly out of repair; but the whole Company were set, immediately, to work; and, after four hours labor, she was placed in the water, at sun-set, apparently almost tight. The Quartermaster furnished us with a pilot; we immediately embarked, with all our establishment of equipage and camp-stores, and committed ourselves to the current of the Niagara, having appointed relays of men to keep the water out of the boat. It soon turned out that our pilot had never been down the river, before, and scarcely knew how to steer a boat. He wished to go down to Chippewa; and thought this a good opportunity.

We knew of no difficulty, however, in navigating the river, except to stop at the proper point; and of this, as the roar of the cataract became audible, we resolved *not to be unmindful*. The night was clear, but dark. We drew cautiously over to the Canada shore, and kept near it, all the way; and, at length, as the increased current indicated our approach to the Rapids, we discovered the lights of the camp, at Chippewa. Some difficulty, encountered in getting round a body of drift wood, at the mouth of the creek, threw us out some distance into the channel, and caused us to drop a little below before we made the shore; but a dozen men leaped into the water, with a line, as soon as we got within their depth; and we were presently brought to, in the still water of the Chippewa. In the mean time, we were challenged by two or three sentinels at once, and a file of men hastily sent to ascertain whom we might be. Satisfied, on that point, however, and report made at Head-quarters, we were welcomed within the cordon of the Army, and made comfortable for the night.

It was just twelve o'clock when our launch was moored; and, within ten minutes from that time, every man, although they had had no refreshment, except a few biscuit, since the preceding morning, was stretched on the ground, or in the boat, fast asleep. Two Staff-officers, at the same time, relinquished to Lieutenant Story and myself what was then deemed the perfection of camp hospitality—to each of us, six feet by one of dry, plank flooring, and an equal area of spread buffalo-skin. It was, indeed, a luxury, though to us not a new one; and, in our duffil cloaks—booted and belted—we soon realized the value of it. And such was our first night's lodging in Canada.

With regard to the positions of the Army: it was found that the main body, on the day just preceding our arrival, had moved forward to Queenston; and the troops among whom we had been received at Chippewa, were the New York and Pennsylvania Volunteers, under General Porter. The morning following, therefore, found my little command again on its feet, with wagons loaded for the remaining march of eight miles to Queenston.

You will judge of the interest which absorbed us, at that time, when I mention that even the great cataract of Niagara, roaring within a few hundred yards of our path, was scarcely an object to be regarded. A brief halt was, indeed, permitted; but scarce a minute allowed for a rapid glance before the drum-taps called every man back to his post; and we were again in full march forward.

But how shall I describe the emotions with which we drank in our first view from Queenston Heights! Standing on the crest of the mountain, near where Brock's monument now stands, the horizon—East, West, and North—was terminated by the silvery surface of Lake Ontario, having its nearest shore in front, about five miles distant. Between that and the foot of the mountain, some three hundred feet below us, lay a varied and beautiful surface of verdure and foliage, intersected by the Niagara-river, running from the abyss of the Rapids, near where we stood, directly out to the lake. But these, beautiful as they were, were not the objects that chiefly engaged our attention. Beneath our feet were a small village and a broad expanse of open plain, adjoining, literally whitened with tents. Long lines of troops were under arms; columns in motion; guards coming in and going out; Divisions of Artillery on drill; videttes of Cavalry at speed; and Aides and Staff-officers, here and there, in earnest movement. There was no great display of gaudy plums or rich trappings; but, in their stead, grey-jackets—close buttoned—plain white belts, steel hilts, and brown muskets; but there were bayonets fixed, and a glance of the eye would show that those boxes were well filled with ball cartridges. There was an earnestness, and with good reason, for, yonder, in plain sight, are the colors of the enemy waving proudly over the ramparts of Fort Niagara and Fort George; and a straggling ray, now and then reflected, tells of bayonets fixed, there, too. This, then, was no mere parade—no stage play, for effect—it was a simple and sublime reality—IT WAS WAR.

A few minutes only could be spared to enjoy this sublime and thrilling spectacle; and we were again in motion, descending the hill; to mingle in the moving groups, below. As an addition to the force, we were received with open arms; and our personal greetings were no less cordial. While the Company was filing in, its position in line was determined and laid out by the proper officer; and, on the following day, half the battering-train was assigned to the Bombardiers, and was fought by them, afterwards, to the end of the Campaign.

And here, for the present, fearful of having trespassed too far upon your indulgence, I suspend my narrative. But, before I take leave, allow me to deprecate your judgment for having occupied so large a portion of your attention in matters of personal interest, and things relating to myself. I assure you I am not so unaware of the foible, sometimes charged—perhaps justly—upon the dotage of the military profession, as not to have guarded myself, generally, against it. And if I have departed, in some degree, from my customary rule, this evening, it is only in obedience to the suggestion of some of your number, in whose judgment, on such matters, I have more reason to confide than in my own. Thus sanctioned, as I have now explained all the external relations of the Campaign and fairly introduced myself as the narrator, I propose, on another occasion, if it meet your approbation, to give, in a simple narrative, the scenes and events following, as they actually presented themselves or became known to me, at the time, beginning with the Battle of Chippewa, although it occurred a few days before my arrival, and ending with the evacuation of the British lines, before Fort Erie, on the nineteenth of September.

The more I reflect upon the incidents of this period, the more sensible I am that, on the part of the community, at large, they have never been rightly understood or duly appreciated. With the exception of the official dispatches—which are always necessarily hurried and concise—and the communications of a few of the officers, nearly all that has been published, in relation to those events, has, in some way or other, from design or otherwise, done them injustice. The British officers seem more disposed to set a proper value upon them than we, ourselves.

It is much to be desired that some means should be taken to retrieve these events from the untoward influences under which they have hitherto rested; and, in as far as I can be instrumental in doing this, my ardent desire, as a lover of my country and my country's service, will be truly gratified.

[TO BE CONTINUED.]

II.—HISTORICAL AND PERSONAL REMINISCENCES OF CHENANGO-COUNTY, NEW YORK.

BY S. S. RANDALL, LL.D., LATE SUPERINTENDENT OF PUBLIC SCHOOLS OF THE CITY OF NEW YORK.

1.—INDIAN OCCUPANCY.

At the commencement of the Revolutionary War, less than a century ago, the entire white population of the State of New York, did not

Vol. II. THIRD SERIES.]　　　AUGUST, 1873.　　　[No. 2.

I.— *REMINISCENCES OF THE CAM-
PAIGN OF 1814, ON THE NIAGARA
FRONTIER.*--CONTINUED FROM PAGE 12.

FROM THE PAPERS OF THE LATE DAVID B. DOUG-
LASS, LL.D., FORMERLY CAPTAIN OF ENGIN-
EERS, U. S. A.; COMMUNICATED BY HIS CHIL-
DREN, FOR PUBLICATION IN THE HISTORICAL
MAGAZINE.

LECTURE SECOND.

In the Lecture of last evening, I attempted to
give a brief outline of the military operations
of the two Campaigns of 1812 and 1813.

My chief object in doing this was to indicate,
precisely, the circumstances which gave rise to
the Niagara Campaign of 1814, and to show how
intimately it was connected with a general plan
for the systematic prosecution of the War, in
Canada ; for there is, probably, no question
connected with the military policy of the War,
which has been so greatly mystified and misrep-
resented as this. The reason can easily be made
apparent. The disappointments and failures of
the preceding Campaign naturally led to great
changes in the *personnel* of the Northern Army ;
and the old officers, who were displaced, scarcely agreeing in anything else, were unanimous in
this, that those who succeeded them were incap-
able of doing anything which would reflect the
least honor on themselves or their country. The
leaven of this ill-feeling was chiefly collected in
the large cities ; and, symbolizing with political
biases of the time, the newspapers, during the
Campaign and for a long time after, were busily
engaged in disparaging every thing connected
with the Army operations, on the northern frontier. The Niagara Campaign, standing conspicuously among these operations, had, of course,
its full share in these detractions. It was said
to have no motive or plan, consistent with
sound military policy : nay, it was diametrically
opposed to such a policy—an absurdity in design, only less monstrous than in execution.
The allegation to which I alluded, in my former
Lecture—that the whole Campaign was the result of a mistake, in the construction of his
Orders, on the part of General Brown—is of a

piece with these slanders ; the whole of which,
collectively, it was my intention to expose by
the narrative then given. If I have been successful in conveying, to the minds of my audience, a just conception of the facts, as they
actually transpired, it will be seen that the Campaign, so memorable, as all admit, for its hard-
fought battles, was no mistake ; on the contrary,
that it was a natural sequence to the operations
of 1813 ; maturely planned, with a wise and
judicious reference, not only to the particular
object, but to the ulterior prosecution and termination of the War.

The official character in which the speaker is
introduced to you demands a word of explanation, as to the relative military duties of the
Corps of Engineers.

All military service is distributed under the
two general heads of executive and administrative. To the executive, belong all the active,
specific military operations—all offensive and
defensive movements, manœuvres, battles, and
the like, of which the results are given in ordinary military dispatches ; and the aggregate
force by which these are performed is called the
Line of the Army. To the administrative,
belong the supply of all the various wants and
exigencies of the operative force, their munitions, provisions, means of transport, clothing
and pay, their drill, discipline, and inspection,
and, generally, whatever is necessary to prepare
them for service and keep them in an active,
healthy, and efficient condition, as an operative
body. The officers assigned to these duties,
from the Line of the Army, having a superior
responsibility, were generally designated, in the
French service, by the word "Major ;" and the
aggregate of officers, so assigned, was called
the "Etat Major"—from which word "Etat,"
by a slight corruption, is derived our word
"Staff." The proper executive and military
services of the Army, then, are performed by
"the Line" of the Army : the subsidiary, though
all important, duties of administration, by "the
Staff."

"The Line" is composed of four different
descriptions of troops, called, severally, "arms
"of service"—Cavalry, Infantry, Artillery, and

Engineers—differing from each other in their weapons and mode of warfare. The first three need no explanation, in these respects, except as they all differ from the fourth : viz, that, while *their* appropriate weapons are, in every instance, transportable, from place to place, those of the Corps of Engineers are strictly local and fixed. They consist of Intrenchments, Breastworks, Batteries, Ramparts, and the like, erected on the ground where they are to be used, either in the attack or defence of positions. Its *material* is thus the result of its own invention, applied to the circumstances of each particular case, with a knowledge of the powers of all other arms, as well as of its own. In European service, this Corps is generally termed the "*Corps du genie;*" and, in our own *Rules and Articles of War*, its functions are spoken of as connected with the highest branch of military science.

But, besides these executive functions, the duties of the Corps of Engineers are also intimately connected with the military administration, or General Staff, of the Army. In all questions, in which the local facilities and capabilities of ground are concerned—such as the formation of Orders of Battle, the disposition of camps, the attack and defence of positions, the forcible passage of rivers, and, frequently, orders of march—in these and other like questions, the chief agent and counsellor of a Commander is his Corps of Engineers.

Such were the relations in which, more than on any previous occasion of the War, this Corps was recognized and employed in the Campaign of which I am speaking. The two Colonels, McRee and Wood, enjoyed, in a high degree, the confidence of the Commander-in-chief, and were in the councils of every movement and plan ; and, it is worthy of remark, to the honor of General Brown, that he was always prompt and explicit in acknowledging his official obligations to them. Under such circumstances, although I was probably the youngest subaltern, save one, in the Army, the department of service with which I was connected, my relations to the General Staff and Head-quarters, and, above all, my confidential intercourse with the Field officers of my Corps, gave me opportunities for the improvement of the Campaign which few officers of my grade could, in any equal degree, have enjoyed. It was my desire, on my arrival at the Quarters of the Army, to have relinquished the command of the Company of Sappers and Miners, distrusting my experience for such a command, in active service ; but there was no Engineer officer intermediate in rank between Colonel Wood and myself ; and the command being restricted, by law, to the Corps of Engineers, I was obliged to waive my objection. Nor had I reason to repent it, afterwards, as it increased my sphere of responsibility and afforded me many valuable opportunities which I could not otherwise have enjoyed.

The Strait of Niagara, on which the Campaign was fought, demands a momentary notice, before I proceed with my narrative. Its length—from Lake Erie, of which it is the outlet, to Lake Ontario, into which it empties—is about thirty miles ; the first seventeen above the Falls being navigable, in connection with Lake Erie, and the last five, below Queenston, in connection with Lake Ontario ; the intermediate distance, embracing the Falls and the upper and lower Rapids, is, of course, not navigable. Beginning at the foot of Lake Erie, about a mile and a half above where the Lake is considered as passing into the river, we have, on our side, Buffalo, the place of rendezvous of the Army, before the opening of the Campaign ; and, nearly opposite to it, on the Canada side, about three miles distant, Fort Erie. Two miles below Buffalo, on the American side, is the present village of Black Rock ; and, about fifteen miles further down, at the head of the Rapids, immediately above the Falls, is the position of the old French trading-post of Fort Schlosser, on our side, and, opposite to it, the little village of Chippewa, at the mouth of the Chippewa-creek, in Canada. From Lake Erie to this point, the river is generally deep and rapid, varying in width from half a mile, at Black Rock, to two miles, at Chippewa ; and containing several islands, one of which, called "Grand-island," embraced between two widely diverging channels, contains nearly thirty square miles of surface. From the village of Chippewa to the Falls, following the road, on the Canada side, is about two and a half miles ; and half a mile further to Lundy's-lane, the site of the battle. The heights of Queenston, on the Canada side, and of Lewiston, on ours, are about five miles still further down, with the villages of the same names, respectively, immediately below. And, finally, at the confluence of the river with Lake Ontario, five miles below Queenston, are situated Fort George and an outwork called Fort Missisauga, both on the Canada side, and Fort Niagara, on ours.

At the opening of the Campaign, on the third of July, Fort Erie was a small unfinished work, occupied by a garrison of about one hundred and fifty or one hundred and sixty men, commanded by a Major. The American Army, in crossing, was organized in two Divisions, one of which landed above the Fort and the other below, while it was yet dark, on the morning of the third ; and having sent a light force of Indians and Volunteers, through the woods, in rear of the work, its pickets were all driven in, and the Fort itself, after a slight show of resistance, surrendered. An American garrison was then placed in it; and, on the foling morning, the advance of the Army, under General Scott, moved down the Niagara and took position, at Street's-creek, about a mile and a half above Chippewa—his front protected by the creek, and his right flank, supported by artillery, resting upon the Niagara—and in this position, he was joined, the same evening, by the Commander-in-chief, with the main body of the Army. General Riall, with a British force, was, at the same time, posted behind a heavy line of intrenchments, below the Chippewa-creek. The situation of the two Armies, then, on the morning of the fifth of July, may be easily apprehended—Chippewa-creek being in front of the British; Street's-creek in front of the Americans; and a level plain, a little more than a mile wide, between the two; bounded by the Niagara-river, on one side, and woods, with occasional patches of low ground, on the other.

The early part of the day passed without any particular hostile movement, on either side. A firing of pickets and scouts occurred, in the woods, on our left, which, a little after noon, became rather spirited; and General Porter was detached, with his Volunteers, about four o'clock, with directions to move, in a circuit, beyond the skirmishing parties, and compel them to retire or, if possible, to intercept them. This he did, as to the movement; but the enemy having obtained notice of his approach, drew back, without his being able to cut them off; and, being strongly reinforced by a corps of embodied Militia and light troops, they presently became, in turn, the attacking party; and the General was compelled to retire.

It soon appeared that the troops, which had thus been thrown forward for the dislodgment of our Volunteers, were a part of the enemy's advance, intended to cover a regular sortie; and that he was now already in motion, across the plain, with his entire force, in order for battle. To receive them, in a becoming manner, General Scott was immediately thrown across Street's-creek, with the First Brigade, consisting of the Ninth, Eleventh, Twenty-second, and Twenty-fifth Regiments of Infantry and Towson's Artillery—the latter taking post near the river, and the former displaying, in order of battle, to the left, with the extreme left thrown forward. It was all done with the promptness and accuracy of a grand review; and the instant the line was displayed, it was engaged with the enemy. The latter was allowed, however, to deliver his fire, several times, and approach to short point-blank distance, without any return. A tremendous fire was then opened, from the whole of our

line, firing with deliberate aim, by word of command—the left, under Colonel Jessup, bearing upon the enemy's right—and, as the enemy were seen to be thrown in some confusion by it, the word was passed to "Cease firing!" "Recover "arms!" and "Charge with the bayonet!"—all which was done with admirable coolness and promptitude, and with an effect which, considering the nature of the troops opposed, it was hardly possible to realize. The columns which had been in full march upon us, but a few moments before, were now, in another brief minute, routed and flying, in uncontrollable disorder, towards the Chippewa.

The coolness and deliberation with which the enemy were received, in this, the first conflict of the Campaign, was a new event for both parties. From ourselves, owing to the circumstances I have mentioned, it has scarcely ever received the commendation to which it was entitled; while British officers, who were in the battle, speak of it in the most enthusiastic terms. "We had "never seen those grey-jackets before," they said. "We supposed it was only a line of Mili- "tia-men; and wondered why you did not run, "at the first fire. We began to doubt, when "we found you stood, firmly, three or four "rounds; and when, at length, in the midst of "our hottest blaze, we saw you 'Port arms' "and advance upon us, we were utterly amazed. "It was clear enough we had something besides "Militia-men to deal with."

General Riall, in his official Report, speaking of the critical point of the action, says, "I im- "mediately moved up the King's Regiment to "the right, while the Royal Scots and the One "hundredth Regiment were directed to charge "the enemy, in front, for which they advanced, "with the greatest gallantry, under a most de- "structive fire. I am sorry to say, however, "in this attempt, they suffered so severely that. "I was obliged to withdraw them, finding their "further efforts against the superior numbers of "the enemy would be unavailing." And what was the superiority in numbers? In another part of his Report, he represents the aggregate force, on our side, at six thousand men; having been augmented, he says, by a very large body of troops, immediately before the commencement of the action; whilst his own force, exclusive of Militia and Indians, is stated at fifteen hundred. Before noticing the battle, in any other respect, let us correct these numbers and present the case as it actually occurred. Our entire aggregate force, in Canada, on the day of the battle, was less than three thousand five hundred men. Of these, the Volunteers were engaged in the woods, with about an equal number of the same description of troops, on the part of the enemy; and these, therefore, may be paired off against each other. A large part of the Artillery was wholly unengaged. General Ripley's Brigade was put in motion, to act on the flank of the enemy, through the woods, and made praiseworthy exertions to do this; but, in point of fact, it did not reach its ground in season, and did not, therefore, take any part in the action. The main battle on *our* part, was fought, then, entirely by General Scott's Brigade and Towson's Artillery, amounting to about one thousand men against one thousand, five hundred. It was a fair trial of nerve and discipline, between these forces; on plain, open ground; without any local advantage or any adventitious circumstance, on either side; and the result was the entire *repulse*, to use no harsher phrase, of the more numerous party.

We claim this result, then, without illiberality, as a fair triumph, on our side; the more signal, as we estimate, highly, the gallantry of the veteran troops opposed to us and the peculiar circumstances under which we met them. Our one thousand, it will be observed, were many of them new in service, and most of them now meeting, for the first time, a disciplined enemy, in the open field. They were hastily displayed, on ground not before occupied by them, with all the moral disadvantage of feeling themselves on the defensive. On the other hand, one thousand, five hundred veteran soldiers, in the highest possible state of discipline—being composed of the Eighth, or King's, Regiment, of the line, the One Hundredth of the line, and the Royal Scots —unsurpassed by any troops in the British Army for bravery or loyalty; the ground chosen, at the option of the British Commander, and with which he was perfectly familiar; and *they*, the assailants. If it had been an appointed combat for trial of strength, between equal parties, what advantage could have been asked, on the adverse side, which was not enjoyed? Yet, with a disparity in the ratio of two to three against us, we were eminently victorious.

The Battle of Chippewa may be called a small affair, and certainly was not, as to the numbers engaged, entitled to the rank of a great battle. It required less generalship, on that account; but the conduct of the troops was, in no respect, inferior; and it is but fair to conclude that the same elements multiplied in any ratio, and as well marshalled, would, with the corresponding disparity of force, have accomplished a similar result. Such was the view taken of it by British officers as well as ourselves. During all the previous Campaigns, no opportunity had occurred so favorable for a trial of strength, in which the victory had not been decidedly on their side, or questionably, at least, on ours. Here there was no room for doubt; the victory against great odds had been fairly

won by us, and now, for the first time, during the War, was it felt that the *esprit du corps* of real service and real discipline had been attained.

The Battle of Chippewa was not more remarkable as the exponent of discipline than as the beginning of a new era, in the mutual confidence and esteem of the opposing forces. They greatly mistake who imagine that such encounters provoke anything like personal animosity or vindictiveness, between the parties concerned. Quite the contrary! The sentiment excited in every generous mind is that of respect and esteem for a brave and loyal enemy—the more decided, as those qualities are more distinctly characterized; and, probably, no persons interested in a state of War are so free from every sentiment of personal hostility as the very combatants themselves. The result of this battle, then, was to awaken a new and far more generous intimacy between the two services, if not between the two Nations, than had ever existed before.

The two days following the battle were employed in opening roads and providing the means for crossing the Chippewa, above the village. The British General, seeing the vigor with which these works were advanced, in spite of his attempts to prevent it, and alarmed for his safety, in flank and rear, as soon as the end should be accomplished, hastily broke up his camp, on the seventh, and retreated down the river. On the ninth of the month, General Brown moved forward, with the main body of the Army, and occupied the camp on the plains of Queenston, where I joined, on the tenth, and where, on the eleventh, he was also joined by the Volunteers having charge of the baggage and stores of the Army, who took post on Queenston-heights.

The week following my arrival in camp, though not marked by any movement of consequence, in the operations of the Army, was, to me, a period of the deepest interest. My local position, in the encampment, was designated and occupied, near Head-quarters, in the centre of a vast semi-circle, on the circumference of which were posted thirteen different Regiments, detachments, and Corps. It would be difficult to transfer, to this peaceful hour and place, an adequate impression of the military sights and sounds which gave animation to the scene. The various guards mounting; the drills and parades; the regimental beats and bugle-calls, converging from so many different points, at once; retreat-beating and parade, at sundown; tattoo, at nine o'clock; and, above all, the fine old spirit-stirring reveille of Baron Steuben, at the earliest dawn of day. These beats commenced, generally, with the Regiment on the extreme right; then the next; the next; and so on; till the whole circumference was one grand chorus of the most thrilling martial music. To some, perhaps, these sounds may be familiar; and a reference to them, in a Lecture, may seem common-place; but few, I presume, who hear me, can have been privileged to hear them in the associations of actual War, in the presence of an enemy, and under circumstances of so much interest as in the case now referred to.

Occasionally, the scene was varied by occurrences of a more particular kind. On the thirteenth of July, a strong reconnoitering party, of several Regiments, with a detachment of Artillery, was seen, under arms, at an early hour in the morning; and, shortly after, moving off, in the direction of Fort George.* A number of officers rode to the heights, to get a view of the scene of action; but, though the smoke of the Artillery was occasionally visible, near Fort George, and a heavy firing heard, the detachment, itself, was hid by the foliage; and we were left in uncertainty as to the nature of the encounter, until its return, at evening. It was then ascertained that the object of the enterprise had been accomplished, the pickets and outposts of the enemy having been beaten back, and the ground examined to within a short distance of the Fort. But the morrow had a tale to tell. The booming of minute-guns, from some battery, on the heights over our heads, and the close roll of the muffled drum, announced the funeral of a General officer, in the camp of the Volunteers—General Swift of the New York Volunteers.

The little Corps of Sappers and Miners, in the mean time, had been armed with a part of the battering-train of artillery; and my own attention was now unceasingly required in distributing and training them for their new duties. From the tenth to the twentieth of the month, with very little intermission, their whole time was employed in the most laborious drills and field-exercises, for which I was fully compensated when the "Marching Order" came out, on the day last mentioned, in contemplating my little Corps, with its long cavalcade, armed, and in complete order, the first in readiness to move.†

The Orders for marching came out on the evening of the eighteenth, but were countermanded, on the following morning. But, on the twentieth, however, the whole force was in motion, at an early hour, in the direction of Fort George; and, at mid-day, we were in position about a mile from the Fort, having our right on the river, and our left thrown back. The distance was so small, that our picket-guards, on the right, were nearly in contact with those of the enemy; and, almost immediately after they were posted, a running fire commenced, between the first two and their opponents, which continued, without any long interval, while we lay in that position.*

The day after our arrival, when this firing was more than ordinarily brisk, I was invited by my friend, Colonel Wood, to join him, in a personal reconnoisance, towards the Fort, as a military exercise, for my own benefit; and, having obtained the permission of the Chief Engineer, we mounted and rode towards the outpost. We passed down the high road, leading to the Fort, under cover of an intervening piece of woods,

---

* The object of a reconnoisance, is to obtain information as to the enemy's position, and force, and disposition, and intentions, and the local resources of the country. This may be accomplished, with sufficient accuracy, under certain circumstances, by only one or two individuals. But, at other times, the object of the reconnoisance can only be obtained by using a heavy detachment, like the one mentioned above.—*Major Douglass.*

† "The whole Army was put under marching orders, "last evening, to move, very early, this morning; and the "Bombardiers had the honor to be the first in readiness,

"being ready to strike their tents before reveille. The "tents were struck about seven o'clock, throughout the "camp. I had all my drivers mounted and every man at "his post, from that time till near eleven, when an Order "came to re-encamp. The marching order is renewed, "this evening; and the same scene is to be acted over "again, to-morrow morning, only with a different catas-"trophe."—*Letter, by Lieutenant Douglass, dated July* 19th, 1814.

July 20th. "It is morning, and one Brigade has just "moved off. It was a glorious sight. The Heavy Artil-"lery will probably move in the course of an hour, and, "with it, of course, my own Corps, and then follows the "remainder of the Army. I wish you could see my pres-"ent line of march. It consists of two very long and "heavy eighteen-pounders, drawn by six horses each; "two caissons, drawn by four horses each; two shot-"wagons, drawn by four horses each; and two two-horse "wagons, loaded with implements and camp equipage. "I have also a good horse for myself."—*Letter from Lieu-tenant Douglass, July* 20, 1814.

* In the arrangements of a camp, in the vicinity of an enemy, small detachments of Infantry or Cavalry, called "Pickets," are thrown out, at various points, beyond the line of the camp sentinels. These pickets are often again divided into small parties, which are thrown still further forward, and which may again be sub-divided into individual guards. In this method, the whole range of country, for one, two, or three miles, in every direction, may be completely under the surveillance of a military encampment. Desertions are prevented; the enemy's reconnoitering parties are intercepted; and, should the enemy appear in force, timely notice is given for his proper reception, while, at the same time, various annoyances may be employed for his obstruction. In the case of a forced reconnoisance, a very strong detachment is sometimes required to beat in these pickets.—*Major Douglass.*

near which our picket No. 1 was posted. As we approached this, we discovered that the firing was chiefly at the second picket, about two hundred yards to the left; and, crossing the fences, we came out into the open fields, in rear of that position, having no longer the cover of woods but the Fort, in full view, before us, at the distance of about half a mile. The field in which we were was full of stumps and trunks of trees, behind which, on the side nearest the Fort, our picket-guard was sheltered; and the next field, in the direction of the Fort, of the same character, was similarly occupied by the picket of the enemy. They were pretty closely engaged, and, of course, our appearance, on horseback, gave increased animation to the fire, on both sides—our picket endeavoring to drive their opponents and divert their attention from us; while the British, on their side, were equally endeavoring to get the best positions and the best aim for hitting us. We, ourselves, kept apart and in motion, moving irregularly, with our eyes chiefly directed upon the Fort; and, though the balls whistled around us, in great numbers, it so happened, miraculously, as I then thought, that neither of us was hit.*

---

* The passing remarks of the lecturer were, we are assured, almost literally the following: "Perhaps you "would like to know how I *felt* when, for the first time, "I heard the balls whistling about me. I have no objec-"tion to telling you. I have heard of a Spaniard who "said he never knew what fear was. Such was not "the case with me. I should like to have had a strong "stone-wall between me and the enemy, for I expected "to be either killed or wounded; and I certainly did not "want to be either. When the close *twitt* of the balls "was particularly sharp and spiteful, I could hardly avoid "putting up my finger, with the impression that the tip "of my ear, at least, must have been touched.

"I may remark, by the way, that many observations "have convinced me how great a mistake it is to imagine "that courage, in a high sense, consists merely in insensi-"bility to danger. So far from this being the case, I af-"firm that true courage may be consistent, not only with "the knowledge, but even with the apprehension, of "danger. The courage, so called, which is utterly blind "to danger, is of a lower order of qualities. It is rather "of a character with the courage of a brute animal, who "does not know nor consider the extent of the opposition "which he shall meet with, and is, certainly, in this re-"spect, insensible to fear. But I am tempted to say that "the man who never knew what fear was, could neither, "on the other hand, realize the greatness of courage. "That is true courage, which advances, in the very face "of danger, even to the cannon's mouth—*not* ignorantly, "but with a full view of all the hazards and responsibili-"ties of the position; *not* because there is no sense of "peril, but because all individual and personal consider-"ations are thrown aside, for the higher claims of a man-"ly responsibility in the path of duty, where *only* true "honor lies."

My attention was presently diverted by my companion calling to me, in a hurried manner, to "*Keep back!*" as they were manœuvering a gun upon us. "Don't let them take us in range," he said; and, raising my eyes to the Fort, it was easy to see that they were preparing to fire. They did not do so, however, probably thinking it not worth while to waste a shot upon either of us, singly; and, after a few moments further delay, we returned to picket No. 1. Here, it was our intention to reconnoitre through the woods; and a couple of videttes having crept cautiously forward, with guns cocked, to see that no lurking foe was secreted in the bushes, we were enabled to penetrate nearly through the coppice. We then betook ourselves to the trees, climbing till we could just see the Fort, at the distance of about seven hundred yards, over the foliage; and, having completed our observations, in about twenty minutes, without interruption, we returned quietly to camp.

An attempt was made by the enemy, in the course of the same day, to reconnoitre us, from the tops of a small schooner which stood a little way up the river, for that purpose. A battery being formed to open upon them, and a fire kindled for heating shot in rear, they became alarmed and immediately dropped down again to their ordinary anchorage. A slight alarm, raised on one of the pickets, on the following morning, brought us to our feet in apprehension of an attack. It amounted to nothing, in fact; but, as it was near daylight, when it occurred, we continued under arms till morning.

On the morning of the twenty-second, we broke up our camp, at Fort George, and moved back again to Queenston; occupying the heights, this time, with the village of Queenston, on the plain, below, as an outpost. My own particular position, in this case, was on the brow of the hill, precisely at the spot since occupied by Brock's monument; and, here, as the view was very commanding, the Staff-officers, particularly the two Colonels of Engineers, were in the habit of making their rendezvous and employing much of their time, during our continuance at that place, in sweeping the horizon of the lake with their glasses. It was the expectation that the fleet might make its appearance, and bring with it an additional supply of battering-guns and other ammunitions, for the attack of the Forts or, possibly, the plan of a combined attack upon Kingston, for which the time appeared not unfavorable.

I allude to this expectation, on our part, as a fact, connected with the operations of the Campaign, and far from intending any reflection as to the grounds upon which it was built or the circumstances which prevented its being realized. No two Commanders, during the War, established higher claims to the esteem and gratitude of their country, than Commodore Chauncey and General Brown; for no two men, within the circle of my own personal intercourse, had I a more entire esteem and regard, while living, or to their memories a more profound respect, when dead. They differed in their views of this co-operation; and who will doubt that, in so doing, *both* of them were guided by pure and patriotic motives? *They*, at least, entertained no such doubt; and, though a temporary cloud did come over their intercourse, at the time, it was dissipated, immediately after the War, and they continued in uninterrupted intimacy and friendship, as long as they both lived.

We remained in our position, on Queenston-heights, until the morning of the twenty-fourth, at which time the expectation of the fleet and every mode of co-operation, in that quarter, was given up. In a conversation, on the preceding morning, I was apprised that the plan of our future operations was about to be changed; the attack upon Fort Niagara and Fort George to be abandoned, for the present; and an attempt made to intercept the enemy's line of communication, round the head of Lake Ontario, by an attack upon Burlington-heights: which, if once occupied by us, and the Lake *also* in our possession, would isolate General Riall's Army, with the forts, and place them, virtually, at our disposal. The execution of this plan, with due caution and effect, made it necessary for a better connection with our depot at Buffalo, to fall back, temporarily, from Queenston-heights to Chippewa; and this movement was accordingly made, on the twenty-fourth, and the ground occupied, on the South side of the Chippewa, fronting northward, with the village in advance.

Such was the state of things, when the circumstances which led to the Battle of Lundy's-lane intervened, and gave a new relation to all our affairs. After the Battle of Chippewa, and during the time we had been manoeuvering on Fort George, General Riall had retired, up the lake, in the direction of Burlington-heights and, there, intrenched himself, at Twelve-mile-creek; but having recently received reinforcements, and learning, as we afterwards found out, that a large addition to his force was at hand, under the command of Lieutenant-general Drummond, he advanced from his secure position, and began, again, to hover in our neighborhood; and, on the twenty-fifth, in the morning, one of his advanced parties was discovered by our picket-guard, in the vicinity of the Falls.

It was on the afternoon of that day—a fine July day, not excessively hot—between five and six o'clock. The Sappers and Miners had just been dismissed from drill. My attention was called to a column, in the act of moving out from the encampment of the First Brigade. My own encampment was on the bank of Chippewa-creek, at the South end of the bridge, between the high-road and the river. As the column approached the bridge, my good friend, Colonel Wood, rode up to me, with a countenance of unusual animation, and gave me an opportunity of learning its object. "The British," he said, "are understood to be crossing "the Niagara, at Queenston, and threatening "a dash up the river, on that side. They are "also in movement, on this side. We wish to "find out what their dispositions are; and the "detachment before us, under the command of "General Scott, is ordered to make a reconnois-"ance and create a diversion, should circum-"stances require; and, if we meet the enemy, "we shall probably feel his pulse." "May I "go with you?" said I. "If McRee will let "you," he replied. Having obtained the approbation of the Chief Engineer, I mounted; and, joining him, we rode forward to the front of the vanguard.

We had proceeded nearly three-fourths of the distance from Chippewa to the Falls without any particular incident, when, in passing round a small coppice of woods, we came in sight of an old dwelling-house, the residence of Mrs. Wilson. There was a number of Cavalry-horses, in the yard, caparisoned and holstered, with one or two mounted Dragoons attending; and, almost at the instant our eyes fell upon them, eight or ten British officers stepped, hastily, from the house and mounted their horses. Some of them rode away briskly; but three or four, after mounting, faced towards us, and surveyed us with their glasses. An elderly officer, of dignified and commanding mien, stationed himself in the middle of the road, a little in advance of his companions, and coolly inspected the head of our column, as it came in sight. They waited until we had approached within perhaps two hundred and fifty yards; and then retreated, slowly, with their glasses scarcely withdrawn, until the leading officer, closing his glass, waived, with his hand, a military salute, which was promptly returned by us, as they all wheeled and rode swiftly away.

During this time, bugle signals were passed, hurriedly, in various directions, through and beyond the woods, to the distance, apparently, of about half a mile beyond the house. Colonel Wood and myself being a little in advance, were first met, at the door, by Mrs. Wilson, who exclaimed, with well-affected concern, "Oh, Sirs! if you had only come a little sooner "you would have caught them all." "Where "are they, and how many?" we asked. "It "is General Riall," she said, "with eight hun-

"dred Regulars, three hundred Militia and "Indians, and two pieces of artillery." General Scott then rode up, with his Staff, and, dismounting, the group of officers entered the house and closely interrogated the woman. When she had given all the information which could be elicited, the eye of the General ran round the circle until it rested upon the person of, perhaps, the most youthful officer present. "Would you be willing to return to camp, Sir?" said he. Not aware of the purport of these words, and doubtful, in my inexperience, whether or no the General wished to test my disposition to sustain the hazard of a conflict, I remained silent. Colonel Wood, however, noticed my embarrassment, and immediately relieved me, by introducing me and saying, "Lieutenant Douglass will, no doubt, be happy "to bear your commands to General Brown." "Very well, Mr. Douglass, return, immediately, "to camp, and tell General Brown that I have "met with a detachment of the enemy, under "General Riall, numbering eight hundred Reg- "ulars, three hundred Militia and Indians, and "two pieces of artillery, and shall engage it, in "battle." I mounted and rode off; but, before I turned the angle of the road, the troops were already beating down the fences and preparing for action.

As I spurred my wearied and foaming horse, over the bridge, at Chippewa, I heard the distant sound of the first firing; and, upon entering the camp, I found myself the object of general and anxious attention. Riding, directly, towards the quarters of the Commander-in-chief, I soon perceived General Brown and Colonel McRee listening to the reports, with very earnest attention. The General led the way to his marque, without a word; then turning—"Well, Sir?" "I left General Scott at "Mrs. Wilson's. He desired me to say that he "has met with a detachment of the enemy, "under General Riall, numbering eight hundred "Regulars, three hundred Militia and Indians, "and two pieces of artillery." "And this fir- "ing?" interposed the General. "General "Scott said that he should immediately engage "with the enemy," I replied. After a few words and comments, with Colonel McRee, Generals Ripley and Porter were instantly ordered to advance and support General Scott. Colonel McRee directed me to return to the field, observing that he would soon follow me; and, in this expectation, I resolved to put myself on the qui vive for him, there.

It must have been at least a quarter past eight, for it was quite dark, when I approached the field of battle, on my return from camp. A little beyond Mrs. Wilson's house—which was brilliantly lighted up, for the accommodation of wounded men—I found the road diverging strongly to the left, through a piece of woods, after passing which, it again inclined to the right; but, directly forward, in front of the opening, there could be traced the dim outline of a hill, occupied by a battery of the enemy's artillery, in full play. It was very easy to see that there were more than two pieces. Several of the shots raked through the opening of the road. They appeared, generally, to pass over my head; but, occasionally, the limbs of trees were cut off by them, and dropped in the way. Here and there, I met parties returning with wounded men. Arriving at the open ground, I discovered the principal part of General Scott's Brigade, on the left of the road, actively engaged with what appeared to be the right wing of the enemy; and I accordingly turned and rode down, in rear of the line, in that direction, nearly to its left; but, not perceiving the officers I was in quest of, and observing, at the same time, some movements on the extreme right, which I had not before noticed, I turned and rode, in that direction, in expectation of finding them, there. As I reached the road, however, one of General Brown's Aids met me, in quest of General Scott; and, soon after, Colonel McRee came up, riding alone, at speed, and it was understood that General Brown and his Staff were not far behind.

"Come," said the Colonel, "let us see what "these fellows are doing;" and, instead of riding down to the left, where the Infantry of the line were chiefly engaged, he spurred forward towards the British battery, to reconnoitre the field. It was now quite dark; but the firing of musketry indicated, plainly enough, the position and extent of the lines engaged; and, having examined these, with great animation, he drew up, at last, at the foot of the knoll on which the battery was posted. After contemplating it, for a few minutes, he turned to me, and raising his hand, he said, with his peculiar emphasis, "That hill is the key of the position, "and must be taken;" and immediately led the way, to meet General Brown.

The General was already near at hand, and rode to the field, in company with the Chief Engineer, who expressed his opinion to him, in the same terms as to me, and entered somewhat more fully into the explanation of them. In the mean time, Colonel Wood joined them, and informed me, a few minutes after, that arrangements had been made to detach the Twenty-first Regiment, under its gallant Colonel, Miller, to storm the height.

I am particular to mention all these circumstances, because the question has been mooted as to who originated the charge upon the British battery, at Lundy's-lane; and particular attempts have been made to attribute the suggestion of this movement to General Ripley. It is, in my view, a subordinate question, altogether; yet, in point of fact, I believe I am correct in saying that it was first suggested to the mind of the Commander-in-chief by Colonel McRee. The storming of the height had been fully discussed and arranged before General Ripley arrived. It was probably ten minutes after all this, before the head of the Second, (General Ripley's) Brigade arrived, through the opening of the woods, on the scene of action; and the order being then taken, the Twenty-first immediately took up its position for storming the height.[*]

And now a word for the Twenty-first and its Colonel, Miller. Colonel Miller—now the venerable General James Miller, for I am happy to say his life is still spared to us—was a rare union of personal excellency of character with a strength and firmness of mind and body, seldom surpassed even in his own Granite State. He had been long in service, having joined the Army with the old Fourth Regiment, under Colonel Boyd, and had been seasoned in every Campaign, from Tippecanoe, downwards. His Regiment was somewhat of the same character with himself; raised, chiefly, in his native State, and devotedly attached to him; and in a fine

state of discipline. A better selection, therefore, could not have been made, for the arduous duty of storming the British battery.

The reply made by him, when it was proposed, was quite characteristic. "Colonel Miller," said the officer, "will you please to form up "your Regiment and storm that height?" He raised his herculean form and fixed his eye, for an instant, intently upon the battery: then turning his bit of tobacco, with great sang-froid, he replied, with a significant nod, "I'll try, Sir!" "Attention—the Twenty-first!" and, immediately, led away this Regiment in the direction required.[*] The other Regiments of the Second Brigade filed along the road and halted, as a right wing to General Scott's Brigade; and, in this direction, the group of officers, with whom I was, moved, also, to avoid being brought in range when the assault upon the battery should take effect. Meantime, the Twenty-first was moved forward, silently and cautiously, but in perfect order, to a fence on the slope of the hill, about forty or fifty yards from the battery, behind which it drew up, in line; and, after pouring one well-directed volley into the battery, they pushed the fence flat before them, and rushed forward with the bayonet. The whole was the work of an instant; the hill was completely cleared of the enemy, in almost as little time as I have been narrating it, and the battery was ours.

Our troops then moved forward, on the right and left, and formed, in Order of Battle, on precisely the ground occupied by the British, at the commencement of the action, only fronting in the opposite direction and having the captured battery in rear. This formation was completed a little after, perhaps half-past, ten. A new moon, which had given a little light, in the early part of the evening, had now gone down; and it was quite dark. Indeed, we had, at no time, after my return from camp, light enough to see the face of our enemy; but it was very evident, from his fires, that he was vastly more numerous than had been represented to us, by Mrs. Wilson; and this we shall be able to account for, presently, by the exhibition of his own Official Report. For the present, it was sufficient for us, that, whatever his numbers were, we had gained possession of his ground; and, although there was no reason to suppose that we should long enjoy it, without opposition, the successful issue of the battle, thus far, gave great animation and confidence to the troops; and enabled them to prepare, with cool-

---

[*] From the rough draft of a letter from the author to the late Hon. John Armstrong: "It will perhaps appear "strange to you that a statement bearing, as you will "perceive, in many of its particulars, upon some of the "questions touching that battle—by which the service "and the community were so much excited, in the year "1815—should have escaped all the investigations of that "period and be now, for the first time, communicated as "matter of history. I will, however, explain this circum- "stance. I was probably the youngest officer in service, "if not in age, in the Battle of Bridgewater; and, feeling "my position to be that of a pupil, it did not occur to "me that anything which was seen or heard by me, in "that battle, was equally, if not better, known to my "superiors in rank.

"It happened, moreover, that the particular agency as- "signed to me, at the eve of the battle, was not stated in "the Official Reports, either of General Scott or of Gen- "eral Brown. Colonel Jones was named as the officer by "whom the first intelligence from the field was brought "to the latter; and, my name not being mentioned, I was "never called upon as a witness. The omission, if it de- "serves to be called by so serious a name, was not, at the "time, considered as of any importance. Before it was "known, the Campaign had already furnished occasions "of higher consideration to myself, personally; and no "motive then existed for calling the attention of those "esteemed commanders to it. After the controversies to "which I have alluded, I regretted not having done so; "but it was then too late to be of use; and the subject "was again suffered to sleep."

[*] It is said that Colonel Miller, himself, first advanced, cautiously, up the hill, alone, to reconnoitre the ground; and, then, returning, gave the necessary directions to his Regiment.—*Major Douglass.*

ness and determination, for the terrible conflict that awaited them.

They were yet but imperfectly formed, on their new ground, when the enemy re-appeared, in great force, as the assailant; and, after a few sharp vollies, given and received, the two lines closed in a desperate conflict with the bayonet.

The bayonet, you can well conceive, is a potent weapon, on the side of high discipline and strong nerves, and, especially, when united with the characteristic determination of the British soldier. The charge of bayonet is not often used, except as a last resort; and then seldom goes beyond the mere crossing of the weapons—one or the other party then breaks or retires. But it was not so, in this instance. It was maintained, on both sides, with an obstinacy of which the history of war furnishes few examples; and, finally, resulted in the second repulse of the enemy. A succession of similar charges—sometimes repelled by counter attacks, upon the flanks of the assailing party, and sometimes by the fire of musketry, in front, in volleys perfectly deafening—were continued, in rapid succession, for nearly an hour, with the same result; until the enemy, having suffered very severely, and wearied with the obstinacy of the combat and hopeless of success, abstained from further attacks, and left us in undisputed possession of the field.

In the meantime, in consequence of wounds received by General Brown and General Scott, the command had devolved upon General Ripley, who, after the termination of the battle, retained quiet possession of the field, for about an hour; and then retired, without the slightest molestation, to the encampment. In one particular only was this movement to be regretted. We had not brought off the captured artillery; and, upon this ground alone, can our antagonist, with any plausibility, dispute with us the palm of this victory.

About the time of the enemy's second attempt to dispossess us of our position, I had been directed to return to camp and prepare my command for action, in case they should be required on the following day. Before leaving the height, I rode around, for the second or third time, among those pieces, to enjoy the satisfaction of seeing and handling them. They were eight in number—brass guns, of the most beautiful model, of different calibres, from six to twenty-four pounders. Not the slightest apprehension came over my mind that I should not, on the following morning, see them all drawn up, on the Camp Parade, at Chippewa; and, even with this assurance, I parted from them not without some reluctance. What, then, think ye, was the bitterness of my disappointment and regret, when I found, on the morning of the twenty-sixth, that the guns had been *left on the field.* Such, however, was the fact. In the absorbing interest of the strife, no one seems to have thought of providing means for getting off or destroying this artillery; and the omission was unfortunately not discovered until it became too late to remedy it.

Irrespective of this circumstance, however, the immediate issue of the battle was in the highest degree honorable and glorious to the American arms. It had been sustained by about five hours hard fighting, and against what disparity let us now examine by a reference to the British official account. It appears that, almost at the moment of commencing the action, General Riall, whose force may have been previously not far from that stated by Mrs. Wilson, had been joined by Lieutenant-general Drummond, with an addition of about one thousand veteran troops, making, with Riall's force, an aggregate of one thousand, eight hundred Regulars, besides three or four hundred Militia and Indians, which are known to have been in this part of the battle; and this was the state of the field, on the British side, from the beginning of the battle until about nine o'clock. On our side, during the same time, it was contested by General Scott's Brigade only, with a small detachment of Artillery, amounting in all to about eight hundred and fifty, say nine hundred, effective men. About nine o'clock, both armies were simultaneously reinforced—ours, by the Brigade of General Ripley, a part of Porter's Volunteers, and some Artillery, in all about thirteen hundred men; that of the enemy by the One hundred and third and One hundred and fourth Regiments, with the balance of the Royal Scots, amounting, by the statement of General Drummond, to about fourteen hundred Regulars, in all—and, as near as can be estimated, the state of the field, including the killed and wounded of the previous fighting, was then a little less than four thousand, on the part of the British, against, at the utmost, not more than twenty-five hundred, on our side; and such it continued to be, through all the subsequent strife, to the end of the battle.

Again; as to the character of the troops and the nature of the position occupied by them. Three of the British Regiments had been detailed from the Peninsular Army; and the others were, probably, not surpassed, in discipline, by any troops of the British service. Being previously on the ground, they were enabled to select their own position, and secure to themselves every local advantage; and it was in the position thus chosen and occupied, that we attacked them. Yet, under all these circumstances—superiority of numbers and position, veteran service, experience, discipline, and *esprit de corps*—his left wing was driven back, with great loss, at the first onset; his right wing only for a time saved from the same fate, by the commanding influence of his battery and the strong position of his light troops, in the woods. Finally, in the second stage of the battle, his battery, the key of his position, was stormed and taken; his whole re-inforced line driven back; his own position occupied and held by us, in spite of the most determined efforts to retake it; and still held in undisputed possession, for nearly two hours, after those efforts had ceased. Will any one say that this was not a victory ?

In the darkness of the night, it is true, we lost sight of the captured artillery; but that event can, in no degree, affect the historic reality of the enemy's complete repulse. It is easily accounted for, by the peculiar circumstances under which the battle was fought and the absorbing interest of the fight. The guns would have been a gratifying evidence of the result; but they are not the only evidence. The facts, as I have stated them, are corroborated by abundant testimony; and the absence of these trophies no more invalidates such testimony, than the absence of an incidental memorandum would impair the validity of a contract or a title similarly avouched.*

---

* The following correspodence will not be without interest in this connection. It is referred to, in a marginal note of the lecturer, and is well authenticated:

"HEAD QUARTERS BUFFALO,
"July 29, 1815.
"To Brev'k Gen Porter &
"Brev'k Gen Miller,
"GENTLEMEN :

"Not a doubt existing on my "mind that the Enemy were defeated and driven from "the field of battle, on the 25th July last, near the Falls "of Niagara, leaving us in peaceable possession of all his "Artillery, I have, on all occasions, so stated.

"Learning that some diversity of opinion has appeared "upon this subject, so interesting to the Army, I have to "request of you, Gentlemen, to state your views regarding "it. You remained on the Field after I had left it, and "know if the Enemy did or did not appear when our "Army marched off, or if a gun was fired, for a consider- "able time before the Army moved, upon its taking up "the line of March, or on its way to Camp.

"I do not enquire of you who were the heroes of the "day, or which of the Corps particularly distinguished "themselves. But I call upon you to vindicate the fair "and honest fame of the Army which has done so much "to exalt our National character. Do not permit its rep- "utation to be tarnished by the faults or follies of its "Commanders. The victory was achieved by Americans "over the best troops of Britain; and the fact being es- "tablished is all that concerns the honor of the country or "the glory of her arms.

"Very respectfully, your obedient servant,
"JAC. BROWN."

The British commander, in accounting for the length and severity of the conflict, quoted the force opposed to him at five thousand men, and gave us credit for a more than ordinary share of gallantry, on that estimate. "It cannot escape "observation," says the annalist of *Dodsley's Annual Register*, in speaking of this battle, "that, although British valour and discipline "were *finally* triumphant, the improvement of "the American troops, in these qualities, was "eminently conspicuous." Such is the language of British historians, on the supposition that our force was five thousand strong. What should be the language of impartial history, when it is verified that we were, in fact, less

---

"BUFFALO, 29th July, 1815.
"SIR :

"In answer to your letter of this date, we have no "hesitation in saying that, in our opinion, the character of "every incident attending the battle of Niagara Falls, "and particularly the mode of its termination, exhibits "clear and unequivocal evidence that it resulted in a de- "cided victory on the part of the American Army.

"We found the enemy in possession of a commanding "eminence, in the centre of open and extensive fields, "without any woods, ravines, or other cover sufficiently "near to favour an attack, and supported by a Battery of "9 pieces of field ordnance. From this position they "were driven at the point of the Bayonet, with the loss "of all his Artillery. After our Army had possessed itself "of their position and Artillery, the Enemy received rein- "forcements, and made not less than three deliberate, "well-arranged, and desperate charges to regain them; in "each of which he was driven back in confusion, with the "loss of many prisoners; but the darkness of the night "and the surrounding woods did not permit our Army to "avail itself, as it might, under other circumstances, of "these repeated successes. The Battle commenced a "little before sunset and terminated a little before or "near eleven o'clock. After the Enemy appeared, the last "time, they exhibited evidences of great confusion by "distant scattering firing in the woods; and our Troops "were drawn up, in great order, on the field of Battle, "forming three sides of a hollow square, with the whole "of our own and the Enemy's Artillery in the centre.

"In this situation we remained for more than an hour, "and in our opinion the Troops were in a condition to act "with more decisive effect than at any former period of "the contest. During this interval, we do not recollect to "have heard a gun, or seen any other indication of the "Enemy being near us; and at the close of it the Army "retired slowly to camp, without any molestation by, or "the appearance of, a foe. We left on the field the En- "emy's Artillery and other trophies of Victory, which "were, at the time of our leaving it, and had been for a "long time before, in our undisputed possession.

"We are, Sir, very respectfully
"Your obt Servants
"PETER B. PORTER.
"JAMES MILLER.

"To Maj Gen'l Brown."

than half that number   And yet there have not been wanting Americans!— shall I not say *recreant* Americans?—who, for the gratification of their personal malevolence, have defamed and disparaged this battle, in almost every particular.

"The darkness of the night, during this ex-"traordinary conflict," I quote, in part, the language of General Drummond, "occasioned "several uncommon incidents—gunners' imple-"ments and accoutrements were interchanged; "British guns limbered up on American limb-"ers, and vice versa." Corps sometimes intermingled friends and enemies, in the strangest confusion. In one instance, a line was seen forming up, in order of battle, supposed to be one of our own Regiments; and an American Staff-officer, riding close up, inquired " What "Regiment is that?"   "The Royal Scots, "Sir," was the prompt reply.   It was by an error similar to this, that General Riall and his whole Staff fell into the hands of the Twenty-fifth Regiment.*

A few minutes before Miller's attack upon the British battery, I was in company with a large number of Staff-officers, in the road, near his right flank, waiting. the result.   We were nearly in the position which had been occupied, in the early part of the battle, by the British Forty-first.   A non-commissioned officer, whose badges and uniform I could not, of course, see, approached me, and with the appropriate salute, recovering his musket, said: "Lieutenant-col-"onel Gordon begs to have the three hundred "men, who are stationed in the lane, below, "sent to him, as quick as possible, for he is "very much pressed."   He was beyond arms-length, and I affected not to hear him distinctly;

* General Riall, with his Staff, was captured by one of Major Jessup's flanking parties, under Captain Ketchum.

It is said that an Aid of General Riall, mistaking the Company for British soldiery, and observing that they obstructed the way, called out, " Make room there, men, for "General Riall." At which Captain Ketchum, seeing a party follow the officer, at the distance of a few horse lengths, promptly responded, " Aye, Aye, Sir;" and suffered the Aid to ride quietly on. As the General, with his Staff, approached, they found the passage intercepted by an armed force, which closed instantly upon them, with fixed bayonets; their bridles were seized; and they were politely requested to dismount. " What does all this " mean?" said the astonished General. " You are pris- ' oners, Sir," was the answer. " But I am General Riall!" he said. " There is no doubt, on that point," replied the Captain; " and I, Sir, am Captain Ketchum, of the United " States Army."

The General, seeing that resistance was useless, quietly surrendered, remarking, in a kind of half soliloquy, " Cap- "tain Ketchum! Ketchum! Well! you *have* caught us! " sure enough!"

whereupon he came nearer and repeated the message.   Much to his astonishment, I seized his musket and drew it over my horse's neck. The man could not comprehend the action. " And what have I done, Sir?   I'm no deserter. " God save the King, and dom the Yankees."

It was past twelve o'clock, at night, when I arrived in camp, and proceeded to make the necessary preparation for the anticipated duties of the following day.   To this end, my own little encampment was changed from the bank of the Niagara to a more commanding position, on the left; my guns placed regularly in battery; the furniture, equipments, and munitions inspected and arranged, for instant service; and, in this attitude, we bivouacked for the night.

The din of battle had ceased, for some time, when the troops returned from the field and, immediately, betook themselves to the rest and refreshment of which it may be supposed they stood greatly in need.   In consequence of the omission to bring off the captured artillery and the deep regret universally felt, on that account, orders were presently issued, by General Brown, to return, with as little delay as possible, to the field; and, at a very early hour, therefore, part of the troops were again in motion, for this purpose.*   The inevitable delays of that movement, however, were such, that the enemy were found already posted on a strong position, near the Falls, when our troops arrived in that neighborhood; and, finding from some prisoners, that further reinforcements had arrived, during the night, General Ripley, after skirmishing with the out-posts, till about eleven o'clock, returned slowly to camp.

[TO BE CONTINUED.]

II.—*AN ESSAY ON THE UNIVERSAL PLENITUDE OF BEING AND ON THE NATURE AND IMMORTALITY OF THE HUMAN SOUL AND ITS AGENCY.*— CONTINUED FROM PAGE 32.

By ETHAN ALLEN, ESQR.

SECTION IV.

Of the natural impossibility of our acting, both necessarily, and freely, in the same action, and at the same time, and of the confusion which attends our reasoning from false analogy.

From the preceeding reasonings, on the nature and agency of the human soul, we may discern, that many perplexing questions may arise, rela-

* There were upwards of seven hundred effective men in camp, whose services in the field of Lundy's-lane had not been called for, and who did not even *see* the action.

"all the other irregularities that these gentlemen "are guilty of, such as selling at false weight "and at false measure, cheating people so out "of one-quarter to one-third of all they buy, is "sufficient reason that their pay should be stop- "ped, and that that they have not drawn of "their salary should be confiscated." "

By a letter from the Marquis de Beauharnois,† Governor of New France, to the Minister, Mar- repas, dated the first of October, 1731, it ap- pears that communications had been received from M. Castin to him, although he did not go to Canada, himself, that year, to the effect that the English were forming considerable estab- lishments in the neighborhood of the Indian ter- ritory, and probably would render themselves masters of it, by force—an opinion which the Governor appears to have entertained, himself.‡

In 1736, the French counted upon two hun- dred warriors, at Penobscot, as connected with the Government of New France ; § and, by a letter from Beauharnois, dated the eighth of October, 1744, they agreed to unite with the French, in an expedition against Annapolis ; and were supplied by him with belts and hatchets.‖

I have not yet been able to find any thing fur- ther relating to the St. Castins, after 1731.

Nothing more is known of Dabadis, than ap- pears in this paper. He evidently is the "Robardee" mentioned by Williamson,* and supposed, by Captain Francis, to have been the son of "Castine, the younger." He, unquestion- ably, was Castin, the younger brother of An- selm : but Anselm must have been the Baron's elder son, who was conspicuous, in Acadie, in the early part of the eighteenth century.

II.—REMINISCENCES OF THE CAM- PAIGN OF 1814, ON THE NIAGARA FRONTIER.—Continued from Page 76.

From the papers of the late David B. Doug- lass, LL.D., formerly Captain of Engin- eers, U. S. A.; communicated by his chil- dren, for publication in The Historical Magazine.

THIRD LECTURE.

In the preceding Lecture, I have brought down the narrative of the Campaign, to the close

* This letter was translated from the French, by Henry M. Prentiss, Esq., of Bangor.
† This was the immediate successor of Vaudreuil. He was a natural son of Louis XIV. He was Governor from 1726 to 1747.
New York Colonial Documents, ix., 991.
Ibid, 1028.
Ibid, 1092, 1107.
‖ Williamson's History of Maine, ii., 71.

of the memorable Battle of Niagara Falls, Bridgewater, or Lundy's lane, including the operations on the morning of the twenty-sixth, till noon. I am now to proceed with the detail of the subsequent movements.

It will be recollected, among the consequences of the recent battle, that, General Brown and General Scott having been wounded, the com- mand in chief had devolved upon General Ripley, and some little change was to be expected, in the military policy of the Campaign. My object in saying this is not to disparage the Commander last named, but to account for a fact.

Change in command, not unfrequently, pro- duces change in the course of action, and so it was, in this case ; and it is interesting to observe, in passing, how, after all, an unseen Providence guides and shapes all our ends, rough hew them how we will. Had the command descended but one step, no one would have apprehended any change in the character of the Campaign, as to enterprise, however many might regret—and, probably, none more than General Scott, to whom the command would have descended—the absence of the cool, deliberate sagacity of General Brown, in the councils of the Army. Had it descended three steps, to General P. B. Porter, very nearly the same result would apply, with nearly the same force. In either case, the question would be, whether the army should be reinforced, on the battle-ground, at the Falls, or occupy its position, at Chippewa. Nor, can it be doubted that, with the aid of the captured artillery, manned and munitioned by us, it would have been in our power to maintain the position, so taken, against any possible assault, on the part of the enemy. Such I happen to know was the unhesitating counsel of General Porter and of one, if not both, of the Field-officers of Engin- eers ; and it was precisely in this policy that I was sent, towards the close of the battle, to pre- pare my command for the exigencies of the fol- lowing day.

In the new state of things, however, a more cautious policy was adopted. General Ripley, having completed the reconnaisances of which I have spoken, on the day following the battle, and returned to camp, determined, not without much opposition from the ablest counsellors of the army, to retire upon Fort Erie, and take po- sition, either at that place or on the heights opposite Black-rock. The Engineers opposing every part of this movement, were understood, of course, to prefer the latter to the former. The final question appears to have been settled in favor of the position at Fort Erie, during the march ; and, about eleven o'clock, on the even- ing of the twenty-sixth, we arrived in the vicin- ity of the fort, and bivouacked for the night. The men slept where and how they could ; and, too tired to be over fastidious, I stretched myself upon the first camp-waggon I saw, which, when I turned up the canvass cover, on the following morning, proved to have been loaded with pickaxes, spades, crowbars, and various other tools and mining implements.

It was foreseen, by those who opposed this movement, that it would be seized upon by the British General, as giving color to an extravagant and unfounded pretension in regard to the recent battle; and so it turned out. In the same dispatch in which he claims the victory, on the field of Niagara, he has endeavored to characterize this movement as the disorderly flight of a beaten army.

"The retreat," says a recent British historian,[*] "was continued to Fort Erie, with "such precipitation, that the whole baggage, "provisions, and camp-equipage were thrown "into the Rapids, and precipitated over the "awful cataract of Niagara!" An awful affair, truly, if it had really happened, anywhere, except in the imagination of the historian. As matter of history, I assure you there is not a particle of truth in it.[†]

The movement, in proper military phrase, would, doubtless, be called a retreat. But it was not a disorderly nor a precipitate retreat. It was not, in any sense, *compulsory*, for we might have lain, any length of time, behind the Chippewa, in spite of the efforts of our enemy to dislodge us. But, in the situation in which we were left, after the battle, diminished in numbers while the enemy had been greatly reinforced, it was thought to be a question, not whether we *could* defend ourselves, but whether we could *protect our depots*, at Buffalo, and our line of communication, at so great a distance from them. In other words, the motive of the retreat was strategical, having regard to the general scheme of operations; not tactical, or evolutionary, having regard to the strength of a certain position or the relative force of the two armies. It was preceded by a forced reconnaissance, on our part, in which the enemy's outposts were driven in, at the distance of almost three miles from our camp. Nor did the British General advance from that position, even as far as the village of Chippewa, till the second day after. There was no pursuit—no hanging upon our flanks or rear—no enemy visible, in any quarter. The march was as quiet as if it had passed through a portion of our own territory. It was undertaken with perfect deliberation, and performed without the slightest disorder, of any kind.

Four days after the battle, General Drummond was reinforced, in addition to all his other reinforcements, with twelve hundred men of De Watteville's Brigade; and *then*, for the first time, he ventured beyond Chippewa bridge. Finally, when he did show himself, at Fort Erie, on the sixth day after the battle, with more than double our numbers, instead of driving us into the lake, at the point of the bayonet, which, consistently with his vain-glorious dispatches he ought certainly to have done, what did he do? He kept at a most respectful distance, beyond cannon-shot, and only approached us in fact with the cautious operations of a regular siege.

It was before superior numbers, then, under a view of general policy, not by defeat or compulsion, that the army retired; and the British General, however he may have stooped to win laurels at our expense, in paper dispatches, showed plainly enough, by his conduct in the field, that the crown of victory was, in reality, none of his.

At the dawn of day, on the morning of the twenty-seventh, I had, for the first time, a survey of our position, of which, by reason of the darkness of the night, I had been prevented taking note, the evening before. The spot on which I stood was a hillock, partly natural and partly formed by the ruins of an old lime-kiln, between the fort and the lake, nearest the latter, eight or ten feet above the water-level, and about as much below the site of the fort. And here I immediately arranged a place for the encampment of my particular command. The different Corps and Regiments began, at the same time, to assume the order of a regular encampment, chiefly on the left of the fort, and extending, from it, towards a high, commanding hillock, called Snake-hill, about half a mile up the Lake, near the shore.

Before I proceed with any detail of events at Fort Erie, allow me to point out the difference between the Fort Erie which I am now to speak and the little work which was taken by us, at the opening of the Campaign. The latter, as I have intimated in my former Lecture, was a small quadrangular fort, partly finished, and not capable of containing a garrison of more than two or three hundred men, at the utmost.

After it fell into our hands, on the third of July, and until the the twenty-sixth, when we returned to it, the American garrison had been engaged in improving and completing its defences, as a mere fort; but, of course, without any idea of the neighboring ground being occupied by the army at large; nor had any works, with reference to such an occupancy, been laid out or contemplated in the labors of the garri-

---

* Allison.

† "It is, indeed, barely possible that some barrels of "bad mess-beef or damaged biscuit may have been "thrown into the Niagara."—*Major Douglass.*

son. The Fort Erie of the siege, now to be spoken of, was rather an intrenched camp, having the proper fort, indeed, for one of its strong points, but extending, for more than half a mile from it, along the lake-shore, with numerous other redoubts and batteries; and embracing an area sufficient for the accommodation of two or three thousand men.[*] With this explanation, I now go back in my narrative to the night of our arrival, when none of these works existed, save Fort Erie, proper.

While the first arrangements were in progress, I had a special duty to perform. One of my guns had broken down, the preceding evening, near Black-rock-ferry; and a detachment of the Company, with a spare limber and plenty of rope and extra draught-horses, was made ready, early in the morning, to go down and bring it in. At the moment of my departure, I was summoned into the presence of the Commandant of Artillery, and severely reprimanded, for having left the gun in that situation. I replied that I had done so by direction of my own Commander, having reported the fact to him, at the time. "Yes," he said, "but if the gun falls into the hands of "the enemy, I have an accountability, too." "That," I said, "is impossible. I put it in the "care of the rear-guard; and, besides, I am just "going down, to bring it in." What peculiar difficulty he saw in this, or whether he was moved by the very juvenile appearance of the speaker, I know not; but he did not hesitate to treat my proposition as absurd and ridiculous; and I left him, meditating *revenge*. Two hours gave it to me. The gun, by that time, was safely brought into camp, weighing about fifty hundred-weights; and, in two hours more, it was safely mounted on another axletree, without the aid of machinery. The Commander came down to see me, at the close of the operation, and very frankly made his acknowledgment, giving me, in the fullest manner, his esteem and confidence, ever after.

On the twenty-eighth and following days of the month, the order of the encampment having been duly adjusted and the troops refreshed, the works of intrenchment were commenced. The ground-plan of a battery, for the extreme right of the position, was traced on the lime-kiln occupied by the Sappers and Miners, and immediately commenced by them. Another, of larger dimensions and in bolder relief, was laid out, on Snake-hill, on the extreme left; and a fatigue party, of several hundred men, was placed under my directions, for *its* construction. The intermediate ground, between Snake-hill and the fort, was, at the same time, laid out in a system of breastworks and batteries, to be thrown up by the Regimental fatigue parties and Artillery, each in front of its respective Regiment and Corps; and a breastwork, also, in front of the Ninth Regiment, between my battery and Fort Erie.

As late as the morning of the thirtieth, the enemy had not yet made his appearance, in our immediate neighborhood. In the course of that day, however, a patrol of British Dragoons was discovered, by one of our scouting-parties, below Black-rock-ferry; and, in the early part of the night following, a larger detachment ascended as far as the ferry, and seized some of the boats which had been left there. It was about the middle of the night, that I was awakened, in my tent, by the Chief Engineer, and informed of this capture, with the caution to be on the alert, as my position was exposed, in the direction of the enemy. He also directed me to place one or two additional guns in the bastion of Fort Erie, commanding the approach, from below. The elevation of the bastion, and the narrow, cramped passage by which it communicated with the fort, rendered this a work of some difficulty. A succession of inclined planes had to be erected. We began the work, however, about one o'clock, with the Sappers and Miners constructing; and, at reveille-beating, two guns were wheeled into their places, in readiness for action.

The approach of the enemy, of course, stimulated our labors, in the trenches; and the soldiers were turned out, almost *en masse*, to work upon them. But it was yet many days before they were sufficiently matured to have given the least hindrance to an attacking enemy; and that General Drummond, with his great superiority of force, did not attack us, in that situation, is only to be accounted for, by assigning to the Battle of Niagara its true character, as a signal and impressive victory, on our part.

It was about the first of August, when the British appeared in force, on the heights opposite Black-rock. On the second, at evening, my own little battery, though not quite finished, was platformed, and the guns mounted. I made my bed on the platform, that night; and, for many weeks afterwards, took no rest, except on the trailed handspikes of one of the guns, with an old tent spread upon them, and wrapped in a horseman's cloak.[*] By great exertions, the battery on the

---

[*] See the accompanying map and description at the end of this Lecture.

[*] In a letter dated "Fort Erie, Sept. 12, 1814," the Lecturer thus speaks of the Douglass Battery:

"I cannot avoid giving you some account of it. It was "originally a sort of arched vault or magazine, raised "above ground, and opening towards the water. In the "course of one night, I dug away one side into a loose "sort of platform, and placed my gun there, having "squared the top a little, so as to give it the appearance of

left was advanced so as to receive a part of its armament, on the third. I was occupied by Towson's Artillery; and was called, afterwards, by his name. On the morning of the same day, the British, for the first time, made their appearance in the edge of the bushes, on the right, within sight of the fort; apparently a reconnoitering party, covered by a body of Indians and light troops. I pointed a couple of guns upon them, and fired the first myself; which was the first gun of a cannonade, which lasted, with very little intermission, from that time to the seventeenth of September, following. The British party was, of course, scattered, immediately, and retreated, with precipitation, under cover of the woods, the Indians making the welkin ring again, with the shrill notes of the war-whoop.

The British had not yet any regular battery to open upon us; but they posted two or three twenty-four-pounders among some sycamore bushes, on a salient point of the lake-shore, below, so as to rake part of our camp and fire into two man-of-war schooners, which were moored opposite. The firing was returned, from my battery, and also from one of the schooners; and, between us, according to the report of the man at the mast-head of the schooner, one of the enemy's guns was dismounted, in the course of the afternoon. †

"a parapet. After one day's brisk cannonade, I found "that I had blown away the earth that remained on the "top, and set fire to the timbers that constituted the arch. "I immediately set the Bombardiers to work; cut away "the logs, entirely; filled up the cavities of the vault; and "formed it into a very decent breastwork. I planked the "platform, also, at the same time. A few days afterwards, "I connected it, on the left, to the breastwork which had "been raised, on that side, by the Ninth Regiment.

"In this state it remained, for some time, until about a "week since (early in September) when I began to devise "some plan to keep the Bombardiers comfortable, as the "nights grew cold; for, hitherto, we had all slept togeth- "er, around the gun. On the right of the platform, the "ground had a considerable descent; and here I set all "hands to work, as near the gun as possible. In a few "days, they had made a sort of cellar, ten feet broad and "twenty feet long, neatly and firmly walled up with sods. "Adjoining this, they dug another similar one, walled in "the same way. I caused the whole to be covered with a "layer of logs; the cracks to be filled up with good "mortar; and a second layer of logs to be placed over "this. The men live in the large part and I in the small- "er. I can enjoy the occasional privilege of a candle, in "the evening; while those who live in tents are obliged to "put out their lights, soon after dark. We are perfectly "secure from any kind of annoyance the enemy can send "against us; and, on the whole, they are considered about "the most comfortable quarters in camp."

† "Aug. 5th, 1814. In the evening, an officer of the "Navy came with some Field-officers of the Army, to see

On the fourth of the month, General Gaines arrived in camp, and took the command; General Ripley remaining as second. The firing, during the fourth, fifth, and sixth of August, on the part of the enemy, was inconsiderable; and we learned that he had thrown himself forward, under cover of the woods, and was there busily engaged in constructing his batteries. We fired upon them, occasionally, to annoy and retard them, as much as possible, in the prosecution of this work; but, of course, it availed little. The first battery was completed and unmasked; and, on the morning of the seventh, a little after sunrise, it opened upon us, with a volley from five pieces, at the distance of about nine hundred yards from our works.

We had heard them cutting, during the night, for the purpose of unmasking this battery; and knew, very well, what we had to expect, in the morning. A little after day-light, therefore, the troops were paraded, with colors, as for a grand field-day; the national standard was displayed at every flag-staff; as soon as the first volley from the enemy was received, the Regimental Bands of the entire army commenced playing the most animating national airs; and, in the midst of it, a salvo of artillery was fired from every piece which could be brought to bear upon the hostile position.

From this time, the cannonade became severe and unremitting, on both sides; and, as the shot of the enemy passed lengthwise, through our camp, it became necessary to dispose the tents in small groups, along the line of the entrenchment, and to erect massive embankments, (called traverses) transversely, for their protection. The most secluded places were selected for the horses and spare carriages of the Park, for the tents of the Hospital department, and for the parade and inspection of the guards. Yet, notwithstanding all these precautions, scarcely a day passed without considerable loss; and the annoyances were incessant. Shots fired with very small charges and great elevations— the ricochet firing of Vauban—were made to fall into the areas between the traverses, and, sometimes, to knock over a whole range of tents, at a single stroke. Others, glancing against accidental obstacles, were thrown off into oblique and transverse directions, producing the same effect. No spot was entirely safe. A Sergeant, under the apparent protection of one of the traverses, was getting himself shaved to go on guard; a chance shot, glancing obliquely, took off his head and the hand of the operator, at

"me, telling me I had made some of the finest shots he "ever saw. This, you may suppose, would make an am- "bitious young soldier feel very vain."—Letter from the Author.

the same moment. These chance shots, how ever, though of frequent occurrence, were not often thus destructive of life, as they occurred mostly in the daytime, when the men were engaged on the works. There, great pains were taken to protect the laborers, by keeping a man on the watch. But, even with all these precautions, the shots often eluded our safeguards, and fell among the working parties, with terrible effect. In spite of it all, however, the works were carried on with vigor and steadiness; and, by the tenth, the battery on Snake-hill—Towson's-battery—was completed and occupied, in full force. The line of breastworks, between Snake-hill and Fort Erie, including two other batteries, was also in a state of forwardness; and the intrenchments of the extreme right, between the fort and my battery, though, from accidental causes, less advanced, were yet capable of making a very considerable resistance. In addition to the intrenchments here spoken of, the extreme left, from Towson's-battery to the water, was closed with a very well constructed abattis;* and a similar construction was added, on some of the more exposed parts of the intrenchment, at other points.

The enemy, in the meanwhile, was still receiving, from time to time, further reinforcements. On the sixth and seventh of August, simultaneously with the opening of their first battery, we were given to understand that two fresh Regiments had joined them, making their aggregate strength a little more than five thousand men; and the expectation was, of course, excited, that we should have a desperate attack, from them, without much further delay. In anticipation of this attack, the men were distributed, for night-service, in three watches; one to be on duty, under arms; and the other two to lie down in their accoutrements, with arms at hand, so as to be ready for action, at a moment's notice. In the batteries, the guns were carefully charged afresh, every evening, with round-shot, grape, or canister, either, or all together, as the case might require; dark lanterns burning; with linstocks and other instruments in their places, ready for instant use. In my own battery, in addition to other missiles, bags of musket-balls had been quilted up, in the frag-

* The Abattis is a defence constructed chiefly of rows of saplings and the tops and large boughs of trees. The ends of the branches are first lopped off, so as to leave stiff points. The trees are then piled with their tops turned from the fortification; and are secured by laying heavy timbers along the rows of trunks. The assailant, therefore, is both exposed to his enemy's fire and obliged to penetrate in the face of these innumerable bristling points, which are often made more impracticable by entwining with them thorns, cat-briars, and the like. —D.B.A.

ments of an old tent, adapted to the calibre of the different pieces, and made ready for use.

A week at length transpired, in this state of expectation and uncertainty—the British frequently exchanging their guns and their men on duty, so as to keep up, without intermission or relaxation, the vigor of their cannonade. On the fourteenth, one of their shells entered a small ammunition-chest, in one of the outworks of Fort Erie, and blew it up. Neither the chest nor its contents were of much consequence to us, though it was to be expected that the enemy, watchful for every advantage, however small, would so regard it; and, accordingly, as soon as the sound of the explosion reached him, it was greeted with three hearty cheers, by his whole line; to which ours, not to be outdone, in anything, immediately responded in three equally hearty. One of their shots, also, a few minutes after, cut away the halyards of one of our flag-staffs and lowered the flag. It was almost instantly restored; but the omen was thought too good a one to pass unnoticed; and three cheers were again given and responded to, in like manner as before. These incidents, and a few others likely to be construed as advantages gained, on the part of the besiegers, gave us a strong assurance that an attack would be attempted, in the course of the following night.

Immediately after nightfall, the lines were all visited by the commanding General, in person, and a special admonition addressed to the officers, of every grade, to be watchful and vigilant, in the certain expectation of an assault. The Chief Engineer and various Staff-officers, also, made the rounds, at later hours, and gave such directions and counsel to the different Commanders, as the occasion seemed to require. "Be prompt "and energetic" was the caution of the Chief Engineer to myself, "for you may be assured "that, whatever else they may do, this will be "one of their points of attack." Thus cautioned, we were not likely to be taken by surprise. The usual proportion of men and a larger than usual proportion of officers were on post, during the night; and the residue, though sleeping, were fully equipped and ready for action.

The early part of the night, after nine o'clock, passed with unusual calmness; and this—doubtless intended to lull us into security—was deemed a further indication of the hostile purpose of the enemy. Midnight at length came; and the hour after was still undisturbed and calm; till, towards two o'clock, it began to be doubtful whether our apprehension had not been excited upon insufficient grounds. I was reclining on my camp-bed, at this hour, and, being somewhat wearied with long watching and strong emotion, I gradually resigned myself to sleep. I was unconscious of the interval that elapsed: it seemed, in sleeping, much longer than it could have been, in fact. But, at length—whether it were a reality or only the confused imagination of a broken dream, I could not, at first, tell—the report of a musket seemed to fall upon my ear, followed by a hurried volley of eight or ten similar reports, immediately after. Whether it were fancy or fact, however, was of little account; my physical energies were roused into action, even before my will was awake; and, by the time I was fairly conscious, I was already on my feet and at my post. Another volley was now distinctly heard, on the far left. It was no dream: the hour of attack had come: and the cry "To arms!" "To arms!" hastily given along the line of tents, awakened the reserve, and brought them into line, in almost as little time as I have employed in narrating.

I think an entire minute could not have elapsed, after the first alarm, before the close double ranks of the Ninth Regiment were formed, upon my left, with bayonets fixed, ready for the battle. My own trusty corps, familiarized, by daily use and constant vigilance, were in their places; the primers had already done their work, and were holding their hands over the priming, to protect it from dampness; while the firemen, opening their dark lanterns, were in the act of lighting their slow matches.

    *   *   *   *

The firing which had given the alarm, was that of the picket-guard, on the extreme left, indicating the approach of the British right column, on that point. The picket-guard, in this instance, behaved well, loading and firing several times with considerable effect, as it retired; so that, by the time it made good its retreat, our troops were in perfect readiness for the reception of the enemy.

The line, from Towson's-battery to the water, was occupied, at this time, by the Twenty-first Regiment, commanded by my gallant friend, Colonel Wood, privileged here, as elsewhere, to be always first in action. About two minutes after, we—on the right—were in our places, the Twenty-first was already hotly engaged with the enemy, and its position, marked by an illumination of exquisite brilliancy, shining far up in the dark, cloudy atmosphere which hung over us; while the battery, on its right, elevated some twenty feet above the level, was lighted up with a blaze of artillery-fires, which gained for it, after that night, the appellation of "*Towson's* "*light-house.*" To the ear, the reports of musketry and artillery were blended together, in one continuous roar, somewhat like the close double drag of a drum, on a grand scale.

. While the battle was thus raging, on the extreme left, a volley of small-arms, followed by a rapid running fire and occasional discharges of artillery, were heard on that part of the intrenchment just South of, and joining the fort, indicating the approach of an enemy, also, on that quarter.

All yet remained quiet in front of us, till the suspense began to be painful, and the inquiry was impatiently made, "Why don't the lazy "rascals make haste!" That they would fail to come, no one, for a moment, entertained the thought. We had seen the signal rockets thrown up, from their right column, at the eve of its approach, and answered from the edge of the woods, in our front; and we knew, as well as they did, what was the meaning of it. The assurance, given by Colonel McRea to myself, that "Whatsoever else they do, *this* will be one "of their points of attack," was, in my mind, almost without the shadow of a doubt, that it was soon to be realized. Yet the intensity of the fire had begun to abate, on the left, and still nothing was heard or seen, in front of us. Hundreds of eyes were gazing intently through the darkness, towards the well known position of the picket-guard, some four hundred yards in advance. Ears were laid to the ground, to catch the first impression of a footfall; but the darkness and the stillness of the night were, as yet, in *our* front, unbroken. At last a sound came—apparently, three or four men, running or walking, quickly, in the direction of the fort. "Who comes there?" was shouted from several voices at once. A slight pause ensued; and then "the picket-guard," was the rather timid reply. I cannot repeat the terrible volley of imprecations to which this announcement gave rise: "Go back to your post, you infamous "cowardly poltroons! Go back! this instant, "or we'll fire upon you." It was, probably, only a few stragglers from the picket-guard, or, at least, not the whole of them; for, within a minute after and long before these men could have reached their position, if they went back, a flash *was* seen, in the proper position of the guard; and the simultaneous report of five or six muskets gave us the signal for which we had been looking so anxiously.

And now were all eyes and ears doubly intent; for we soon began to hear the measured tread of the dense columns, approaching; the suppressed voices of the officers giving words of command and caution—"Close up "—"Steady! "men—"Steady! men "—"Steel "—"Captain "Steel's Company "—and other like words, the meaning of which I shall explain, presently. A brief pause being still permitted, for the retreat of the picket-guard, the darkness and silence of the night were *darkness* and *silence* no longer.

At a given instant, as if by a concerted signal, the fires broke forth; and were immediately in full play, along the whole line of batteries and intrenchments, from the water to the fort, inclusive.

* * * *

It was now near *three* o'clock. The firing had greatly abated, on the further left; and it was soon understood that the enemy's column had been repulsed, at all points, on that quarter. Their attack had been chiefly confined to the abattis, between Towson's-battery and the water, defended, as I have remarked, by the Twenty-first Regiment and the artillery of Towson's-battery; and, though conducted with great gallantry, and long persevered in, it was steadily and constantly repulsed. The enemy had been rallied, several times, and brought back to the assault, after being repulsed; but always with the same result. In the darkness of the night, they tried to deceive our people into a belief that they were firing upon their own men. A part of the column even waded out into the lake, to get around the left flank of the abattis; but the Twenty-first was ready for them, and received them, as prisoners, as fast as they reached the shore—finally, an offensive movement, on our part, threatening the flank of the attacking party, completed their repulse; and, after a running fight, of short duration, the ground in front of the Twenty-first was restored to our possession, and the picket-guard reposted.

The firing, on the immediate left of the fort, had also begun to subside at the period of the action to which we have now arrived. It was, in fact, a mere feint—an expedient, on the part of the enemy, to deceive us as to his real point of attack. The interest of the whole battle was now, therefore, transferred to Fort Erie, proper, and the extreme right. These points had been approached by the enemy, in two columns—one, moving on the level of the esplanade of the fort, for the attack of that work; and the other, along the lake-shore, on the level of my battery. The first was received by the artillery-fires of the fort and detachments of the Nineteenth and Rifle Regiments, stationed in and about it—too small an amount of musketry, doubtless, for the occasion, as we shall presently notice—the second, by the guns of my battery, with the musketry of a detachment of New York Volunteers, on the right, and of the Ninth Regiment on the left.

The darkness of the night prevented us seeing the precise effect of our fires; but the ground was familiar to us, and we had no difficulty in giving the proper elevation and direction to the guns. The cannon were loaded, habitually, for short quarters. They were filled with round-shot, grape, canister, and bags of musket-balls, at discretion, till I could touch the last wad, with my hand, in the muzzle of the piece.

The firing, on our part, had continued in this way, for some time; when a mysterious and confused sound of tumult, in the salient bastion of the fort, just above us, was followed by the cessation of the artillery-fires, at that point: and presently a command was addressed to us, on the level below, by some one on the platform, calling, in a loud voice and tone of authority, "Cease firing! You're firing upon your own "men." The foreignness of the accent, however, betrayed the person and purpose of the speaker. The firing did, indeed, slacken, for a moment, and the column, in front, as we afterwards learned, was about to take advantage of it; but the reaction was short. Another voice was presently heard above the tumult, commanding, in a different strain, and with no foreign accent— "Go to H—. Fire away there, why don't you?" and so we did, with more animation than ever. Some of the guns of the bastion being charged with grape-shot, were then turned and fired upon us, and a rambling fire of musketry was kept up, for a short time, from the same point; all indicating that the bastion had most surely been carried, and was now in the hands of the enemy. An old stone building, however, overlooked the bastion, and separated it from the inner fortifications, by a narrow passage, which the enemy could not penetrate. A detachment of the Nineteenth Infantry had been stationed in this building; and we now saw, by the increased animation of the fires, from the windows and loop-holes of the second story, that it had been reinforced, for the purpose of reacting against the enemy, in the bastion.

A firing was heard, at the same time, from a remoter part of the interior of the fort; playing, with great animation, for a while, and then ceasing; and so, with varied intensity, for some time. It was evident that a strife of no common sort was going on, in that quarter, but with what effect, our engagements in front did not permit us to enquire.

Nearly an hour elapsed, in this kind of warfare: vollies of musketry, with an occasional clang of other weapons, within the fort; while the line with which I was particularly connected was hotly engaged with the enemy's column, in front. The aim of this last was to pass our breast-works, with scaling-ladders, or to penetrate the open spaces; and, though he had not succeeded in reaching these points, we had reason to know that he had, several times, renewed the attempt, and was only, in fact, finally repulsed, as the day began to dawn. The remnants of this column then joined the British reserve, near the woods; and the guns of the "Douglass Battery" were turned so as to rake across the salient point of the contested bastion, to intercept communications or succors. The bastion itself was still in the possession of the enemy; but it was understood that they were not only unable to penetrate further, but that they had been terribly cut up by the fires from the block-house and other adjacent parts of the fort and outworks.

Several charges had been made upon them; but, owing to the narrowness of the passage and the height of the platform, they had, as yet, been unsuccessful. Another party, however, it was said, of picked men, was now just organized, with the hope of a better result. To this enterprise, then—the only thing now remaining to complete the repulse of the enemy—the attention of every beholder was most anxiously bent. The firing within the fort had already begun to slacken, as if to give place to the charging-party: the next moment was to give us the clang of weapons, in deadly strife. But, suddenly, every sound was hushed by the sense of an unnatural tremor, beneath our feet, like the first heave of an earthquake; and, almost at the same instant, the centre of the bastion burst up, with a terrific explosion; and a jet of flame, mingled with fragments of timber, earth, stone, and bodies of men, rose, to the height of one or two hundred feet, in the air, and fell, in a shower of ruins, to a great distance, all around. One of my men was killed by the falling timber.

* 　　* 　　* 　　* 　　*

The battle is over; the day had now fully broke; but, oh God! what a scene! At every point where the battle had raged, were strewed the melancholy vestiges of the recent terrible conflict. There is the ruined bastion, the scene of such desperate strife, smoking with the recent explosion, and, all around it, the ground covered with the bodies of the dead and wounded—the former in every stage and state of mutilation. Near the bastion, lay the dead body of a noble looking man, Colonel Drummond, the leader of the British charge, at that point: his countenance was stern, fixed, and commanding, in death. In front of our fires, between the bastion and the water, the ground was literally *piled* with dead. Within forty yards of my battery, a sword was found and handed me, still attached to the belt, which was stained with blood, and evidently had been cut away from the body of the owner, who could not be found and probably had been carried off the field. Of his rank, therefore, we could but conjecture; though the peculiarity of its shape and workmanship has since led me to suppose that it might have belonged to the leader of the One hundred and third Regiment, Colonel Scott, who was killed at the head of the enemy's left column.*

It became my duty, as an Engineer, to overhaul and repair the ruins; and, as soon as the action was decided, I was called upon to re-lay the platform of the ruined bastion. The whole bastion and its immediate neighborhood were heaped with dead and desperately wounded; while bodies and fragments of bodies were scattered on the ground, in every direction. More than a hundred bodies were removed from the ruin, before I could proceed with the work; and, soon after, to heighten the misery of the scene, it began to rain, violently.

Several hours were employed in carefully disengaging the wounded and burnt from the ruins: those who were yet alive were sent to the care of the Army Surgeons; while the dead bodies were passed over the embankment. While the repairs were in progress, the parties detailed for the purpose excavated large graves, a little distance without the fortification, and gathered the dead, who were buried, forty and fifty together, side by side, with the honors of War. How little do those who quietly read the papers know of the real calamities of War!

It is not difficult to account for the cause of the explosion, in the bastion. The magazine [*ammunition-chest?*] was under the platform, and quite open. In the haste and ardor with which the guns were served, during the action, and in the confusion of the *melée*, some cartridges were doubtless broken and the powder strewed around, forming a train, or succession of trains, connecting with the magazine, which a burning wad or the discharge of a musket might easily ignite. As to its effect in deciding the contest, it was very small, if anything. The British General found it very convenient to assign the explosion as the chief cause of the failure of the enterprise; but he had been completely repulsed, with dreadful carnage, at all points, *before* the explosion. The British troops, in the bastion, were unable to advance, one step. Their Commander was killed. Their numbers were momentarily thinned, by our fires; and so completely were they cut up and disabled, that, of those removed from the ruins of the bastion, but a very few were free from severe gunshot wounds. Indeed, had the explosion been a few minutes later, the whole of their reserve would probably have been intercepted and cut off, by a strong detachment, which was in motion, for that purpose.

The loss of the enemy, by this engagement, in killed, wounded, and prisoners, could not have been less than eleven to twelve hundred. Nine

---

* The sword is still in the possession of the lecturer's family. The hilt is a plain but serviceable one; the blade is very much curved, and handsomely worked with the arms and shields of England, Scotland, and Ireland. A scroll work, near the hilt, is inscribed with "THE 103RD REGIMENT."

hundred and five is the loss, according to their own official returns, which do not name the De Wattevilles, who are known to have lost from two hundred to three hundred, at least. The loss, on our side, was, certainly, not over fifty, in killed and wounded.

The following is the "Secret General Order of "Lieutenant-general Drummond," issued on the eve of the battle :

" SECRET GENERAL ORDER OF L[t] GEN[a] DRUM-
"MOND.

" HEAD QUARTERS, CAMP BEFORE FORT ERIE.
"Aug 14, 1814.

" *Order of Attack.*

' RIGHT COLUMN. *Lieutenant-colonel Fischer*,
"to attack the left of the enemy's po-
"sition. Eighth, or King's Regi-
"ment; Detachment of DeWatte-
"ville's; Light Companies of the
"Eighty - ninth and One hundredth
"Regiments ;* Detachments of Royal
"Artillery, with Rockets; Captain
"Eustace's Picquet of Cavalry;
"Captain Powell, Deputy Assistant-
"quartermaster-general.

" CENTER COLUMN. *Lieutenant-colonel Drum-*
"mond. Flank Companies of the
"Forty-first and One hundred and
"fourth Regiments; Detachment
"of fifty Royal Marines; ditto of
"ninety Seamen; ditto of Royal
"Artillery. Captain Barney, Eighty-
"ninth Regiment,† will guide this
"column, which is to attack the Fort.

" LEFT COLUMN. *Colonel Scott.* One hundred
"and third Regiment‡; Captain El-
"liott, Deputy quarter-master-general,
"will conduct this column, which will
"attack the right of the enemy's posi-
"tion, towards the lake, and endeav-
"our to penetrate by the openings, us-
"ing the short ladders, at the same
"time, to pass the intrenchment, which
"is reported to be defended only by
"the enemy's Ninth Regiment, two
"hundred and fifty strong.

" The Infantry Picquets, on Buck's Road, will "be pushed on, with the Indians, and attack "the enemy's picquets, on that road. Lieutenant "W. Nicholl, Quarter-master-general of Militia, "will conduct this column.

"The rest of the troops, viz., the First "Battalion Royals; the remainder of the De "Watteville's; the Glengary Light Infantry; "and Incorporated Militia, will remain in re-

* About eleven hundred men.
† Say about seven hundred men.
‡ About seven hundred and fifty men.

"-erve, under Lieutenant-colonel Tucker and "κ. to be posted on the ground at present oc- "cupied by our picquets and covering parties.

"The Squadron of Nineteenth Light Dra-
"goons will be stationed in the ravine, in rear
"of the battery nearest the advance, ready to
"receive charge of prisoners and conduct them
"to the rear.

"The Lieutenant general will station himself "at or near the battery; where Reports are to "be made to him.

"Lieutenant-colonel Fischer, commanding "the right column, will follow the instructions "which he has received; copies of which are "communicated to Colonel Scott and Lieutenant- "colonel Drummond, for their guidance.

"The Lieutenant-general most strongly re-
"commends a free use of the bayonet. The
"enemy's force does not exceed fifteen hundred
"men, fit for duty; and these are represented
"as much dispirited.

"The grounds on which the columns of at- "tack are to be formed, will be pointed out, "and the orders for their advance given, by the "Lieutenant-general commanding.

" *Parole*, Steele. *Countersign*, Twenty.

" J. HARVEY. D. A. General."

The British General speaks disparagingly of our little force, and evidently contemplated an easy victory, at the point of the bayonet; but his tone was wonderfully changed, when he afterwards comes to sum up the materials for his Official Despatch. The fifteen hundred dispirited soldiers, not more than half of them having been really engaged, had repelled, with immense loss, all the columns of attack; and, though they were doubtless indebted, in no small degree, to their entrenchments, for this result, these very entrenchments were the creation of the army who defended them; having sprung into existence, within the last fortnight, in the face and under the fires of the same enemy by whom they were now attacked.

In the same ratio in which this result was mortifying to them, it was gratifying and encouraging to us. The troops, who had really been somewhat dispirited, were immediately restored to cheerfulness and confidence; nor were these feelings again subdued, during all the labors and privations of the subsequent siege.

The sensation produced in the neighbring Counties, on our side of the line, was no less remarkable. The inhabitants had been disheartened, as well as ourselves, by the defensive attitude to which we had been reduced. As far as our cannon were heard, even upon the Ohio lake-shore, the most excited apprehensions were felt for our safety; and the reaction among them, after the result of this battle was fully known, was equally interesting, in itself, as it was fruitful in kind offices for our personal comfort and relief. In a very short time, they begun to venture over, in boats, from Buffalo; and, thus familiarized, an intercourse was afterwards kept up, which enabled us to obtain occasional supplies of fresh provisions, of which we were greatly in need.*

The losses of the enemy, in this assault, were so severe, that we were permitted to enjoy a few days of comparative rest from the fires of his artillery; and the interval was diligently improved by us, after repairing the bastion, in completing the residue of the defences, along the line of our intrenchment. The attack had made us aware of our weak points; and we lost no time in improving our experience. All unnecessary openings were closed; the abattis renewed; the intrenchments generally strengthened, at every exposed point; new defences were projected around Fort Erie; and ground broken, with a view to complete the unfinished batteries, in rear.

The enemy, during this time, were not idle—although they did not fire much upon us, they were evidently engaged, under cover of the woods, in extending and throwing forward their intrenchments, to the right of their first battery; and, on the morning of the nineteenth, they unmasked their battery, No. 2, more elevated, and nearer, by two or three hundred yards, than the first. It was armed with four heavy guns and an eight-inch howitzer. Its fires were chiefly directed against our working-parties, on the new bastions of Fort Erie; while the guns of the first battery and two heavy mortars, now for the first time opened upon us, were used for the annoyance of the camp, generally. By the twenty-first, the cannonade from these two batteries was in full play, with a vivacity far exceeding anything we had before experienced, not only in the number of the guns, but in the activity with which they were served.

It will, perhaps, meet the interest of this occasion, at least, of the unmilitary portion of my hearers, to state a little more particularly the nature of these annoyances and the kinds of missiles which, at this time and for many weeks afterwards, were thrown among us, at the rate of one or two hundred—sometimes four or five hundred—per diem.

The chief firing was, of course, from heavy

* Our usual meals consisted of salt pork, raw, and salt pork, fried, served up on barrel-heads and staves, with biscuit and stale bread. The "varieties" of our camp bill of fare were salt butter, at four to six shillings per pound; heavy sour bread, at three shillings; perhaps some onions and potatoes, at two or three dollars per bushel; meagre wine, concocted of logwood and vinegar, with an infusion of gall nuts; and *cookery* as we could catch it.

cannon, of the calibres of twelve, eighteen, and twenty-four pounders, loaded with ordinary round-shot. Nine pieces of these were in play, from the two batteries mentioned, and four added, afterwards. The shot were fired direct and in ricochet, reaching almost every part of the camp, so that the most retired and secluded places scarcely afforded protection to the troops in guard-mounting and other parades.

A column, or a guard of no more than two or three files, sometimes a *single person*, on horseback, in certain parts of the camp, drew one or more shots from the British batteries. The smallest gleam of light, in a dark night, produced the same effect; so that it became necessary to prohibit, in Orders, all lights, after dark. I had just crept, one evening, under an old tent that leaned against the ruins of a stone house, in rear of my gun, when Colonel Aspinwall, of the Ninth Regiment, came softly to me, and roused me with the agreeable intelligence that he had brought a letter for me. I had a dark lanthern burning under the gun, to which I hastened; and, having opened it but a straw's width, I broke the seal and passed my letter, backwards and forwards, before the dim light, to catch the signature and the nature of its contents. The night, however, was somewhat misty, and the single gleam of light which faintly illuminated a small portion of the damp and ruined stone wall, did not pass unnoticed. I had barely stretched myself out again to rest, when an eighteen-pound shot came rushing past the gun I had just quitted, and tore directly through the wall under which I was lying. In a very short time the more exposed parts of the camp were thus completely ploughed up. Many of the tents were pierced with shot-holes; and some of them, on the right—my own among the number—were literally shot to rags. Scarcely a day passed without some hair-breadth escapes, and other like memorabilia, more or less wonderful. It was said that one of our officers being thirsty, in the night, raised himself up to reach a pitcher of water; and when in that position, a shot passed through his tent and carried away his pillow.

One day, about dinner-time, at Head-quarters, while Colonels McRea and Wood and other officers were seated around the mess-table, great tumult and confusion were heard in the next apartment, which was used as the kitchen, followed by a ripping and tearing of the timbers, nearly under their feet; and, upon inquiry, it appears that a round-shot had passed through the back of the chimney-place, killed one of the cooks, and somewhat disordered the cooking utensils. The line of direction would have carried it precisely upon Colonel Wood, but these various obstacles served to glance the ball towards the lower edge of the partition, where it entered the floor, and, cutting through a few timbers, dropped into the cellar. Upon one occasion, a twenty-four-pound shot came tearing along so close that I felt its unwelcome breath. It passed by and shivered to pieces a heavy cedar picket, which stood a few feet off; picking up some of the fragments, I threw them into my sleeping quarters. Upon opening my baggage, at West Point, some time after, I found that they had been wrapped up by my soldier-servant, in the fragments of my old tent; and, on handing them over to the joiner, he contrived to make me a very serviceable chess-board, using the cedar for the dark squares. Observing a group, one day, gathered round a wounded man, I presently joined it. A round-shot had carried away part of his left side. Life was ebbing surely away; but, as is usual, in such cases, the wound was attended with little pain. He was dictating, with great calmness and emphasis, a few words for his absent friends—"Tell them," he repeated, at intervals, "Tell them that I " died like a brave man, doing my duty in de-" fence of my country." While in the act of repeating this charge, he expired. Some of the occurrences were of a less serious character. A subaltern of the Eleventh, a good humored Hibernian, on returning to his tent, after being on fatigue, all day, found that a shot had passed through the tent and cut off the skirts of his uniform coat. He immediately seized the remaining part, by the collar, and brought it out to show his brother officers what a narrow escape he had had, as he had been "on the "point," he said, "of putting on that same "coat, in the morning !"*

* I remember having heard the lecturer relate another anecdote of this same individual.

It seems he was famous for telling wonderful stories of what he had heard and seen, and was particularly fond of magnifying the things of the "owld country," above anything which could be found in the "new." One of his military friends took a convenient opportunity to tell him that he would lose all character for truth, and nobody would believe him if he continued this habit, much longer; and the bargain was made between them that, whenever "Jem" was on the point of committing himself to a rash assertion, the friend should pinch him, or hit him, or touch his foot, to put him on his guard.

It happened, soon after, that the conversation at the mess-table turned upon the subject of barns. "Umph!" said Jemmy, "the barns in this country are nothing to the "barns in Ireland! nothin' at all! I knew one of a barn "on an estate in our neighborhood." Here his friend touched his foot, and Jemmy closed his mouth. "Why, "Jemmy, what was that? tell us about it," called out half a dozen voices. "How large was it?" "How large did

¹ HIST. MAG. VOL. II. 10.

Another of our annoyances was from the bomb-shells. These could be avoided without much difficulty, if one had time to attend to them; but as this could not always be done, they were, sometimes, particularly in the working-parties, very destructive. Colonel McRea, with Major Trimble, was one day inspecting my work, at the new bastion, when a discharge was observed at the British mortar-battery, and an officer in company remarked that the shell was falling precisely in the bastion where we were. We eluded it, however, though with some difficulty, by retreating to the further side of a row of heavy palisades.

It was by a missile of this kind that, on the eighth or ninth of September, General Gaines, with some Staff-officers, in the house occupied as Head-quarters, was severely wounded. I happened to be on the rampart of the new bastion, at the time, and traced the flight of the shell, as it passed over my head, until it descended through the roof of the building. The General was writing, at the time. It passed down, near his right hand, into the cellar and instantly exploded.

Another kind of missile was called the shrapnel shell—so called from its inventor, Colonel Shrapnel of the British Army. It is a thinner cast-iron shell than the bomb-shell, and is filled with bullets, etc., etc.; and the interstices are filled up with gunpowder. It is projected, like a round-shot, from a piece of ordnance called a howitzer. The contents are often exceedingly destructive. When the shell explodes, they sometimes scatter in every direction: sometimes they are thrown together, in one mass. I have seen the bullets of one of these shrapnel-shells strike the side of a firmly imbedded rock, and, breaking into minute fragments, fall to the ground, in a shower of silver flakes.

Finally the congreve rocket, which, however, served only to frighten a few horses and set fire to a tent or two, although our enemy seemed to set a high value upon its destructive powers. For it happened, one day, at the same time that a number of British Dragoons

"you say?" replied Jemmy, forgetting the admonition. "How large! Why, it must have been sex thousand foot "long, and upwards." A roar of laughter ensued, during which the friend contrived to grind his toe with great emphasis. As Jemmy started back, some one called out to know how wide that barn was. "How wide!" piteously answered Jemmy, who was inspecting his bruised member, "Oh, dear! it was sex foot." Hereupon the laughter was very loud and long; and Jemmy, losing patience, turned wrathfully upon his considerate friend—"See "there, now—ye've made me a greater fool than ever, for "if ye had'nt trod so hard on my toe, I'd have squared "the barn."—Rev. Malcolm Douglass, D.D.

were seen riding to a distant part of the shore, to water their horses, an Artillery-officer came down to my battery, to experiment with some of these rockets, of his own manufacture. But, though they scarcely reached half the distance, no sooner did the Dragoons hear the rush of the rocket than they turned their horses' heads, and scampered off, out of reach of all missiles.

Such were some of the modes of warfare with which we had to contend; and such a few of the occurrences among us, from the twentieth of August to the seventeenth of September.* But it is amazing to see how soon men may be familiarized, even to such forms of imminent danger. After the first week, although fifteen or twenty men were frequently carried off in a day, from the fatigue-party, in the bastion, the works went on, without any visible interruption, and with no dread of danger, in comparison with that of the incessant severe labor. The soldier-boys of the camp were seen constantly running races with spent balls and throwing stones at a bomb-shell, just ready to explode, in much the same spirit as we see them, sometimes, stoning a hornet's-nest.

The British, in the mean time, were extending their works also in the woods, further round to their right; and, early in the month of September, we had reason to believe they were preparing a *third* battery for us, on the salient of the new bastion. With a view to retard this work as much as possible, their position was reconnoitered and a lantern hung in the edge of the woods to give the direction to our gunners. A vast number of shot were

* Amongst some detached papers in the original manuscript, I find the following note: "Meantime, however, "our works went steadily on. The intrenchments, where-"ever they had not been previously finished, were form-"ed up and arranged, in the best possible manner for de-"fence. On many parts of the line, where there was any "exposure to attack, pikes of a rude construction were "prepared, by fitting rejected bayonets on poles of suffic-"ient length to reach over the parapet, to be used against "the enemy, in case he attempted to scale. The line of "abatis was, at the same time, completed around the en-"tire work, and, at all exposed points, was rendered more "impenetrable than ever. One night, a deserter from the "enemy became somehow entangled in it and remained "several hours without the power to extricate himself; "and when, after calling piteously for release, he was, "at last, taken out, with the assistance of some of our "men, his clothes were, for the most part, triumphantly "retained by the relentless thorns and briers of the abat-"tis. Our ability to repel attack became every day more "and more apparent; but the enemy, unfortunately, gave "us no further opportunity of testing it. He seemed to "have had enough of personal encounter, and aimed only "to cripple us or tire us out, by the fires of his artillery."

thrown; but the battery was nevertheless unmasked, and opened upon us, at the distance of five hundred yards, early in September.*

The completion of our bastions, now elevated fourteen or fifteen feet above the esplanade, in the face of these accumulated fires, became a work of great difficulty and exposure. Much of it had to be done in the night; and it took, therefore, nearly two weeks in September to do what could, otherwise, have been done in five or six days. It was finally completed, and the guns mounted, ready for action, on the fifteenth.

While the strife was thus going on, on the part of the Artillery and Engineers, the Infantry, in addition to their extreme fatigue-duties, were almost daily engaged in skirmishing-parties with the picket-guards and parties of the enemy. In these affairs, we almost always gave the lead; for such was the general desire to draw the enemy into battle, that officers and men were always ready to volunteer for such enterprises. We had now been many weeks exposed to a galling cannonade, and had become heartily tired of the annoyances and inconveniences of this condition. We knew they had recently received reinforcements; our defences were very complete; and, by the middle of September, no hope was more ardently cherished than that they would come and attack us again. Many a morning, from two o'clock till day light, have I stood on my battery—a dozen

* "The soldiers now, since the assault, work with alacri-"ty, and the works are making astonishing progress. De-"sertions have indeed taken place, but comparatively very "few, and for a few days past, none. They, on the other "hand, are flocking over to us, in great numbers; no less "than eleven have come in this day, among whom is one "Royal Scot, a most remarkable circumstance. The in-"formation they bring is rather amusing. They say they "had finished a new battery in the woods, and got it in "readiness to open (this we knew). But when they came "to cut away the bushes and trees, they found it *would "not work;* and they were obliged to commence *r..ding* "in a different situation. This I must acknowledge is "going upon true *a-posteriori* principles; but, at the same "time, I should hardly suppose an officer of the Royal En-"gineers would adopt this mode of proceeding, so far as "to build his battery first, and *then* try if it would an-"swer his purpose.* I should hardly do worse, myself. I "had almost forgotten to tell you, that General Brown, by "some masterly manœuvre, had intercepted the British "mail, and made himself master of some interesting doc-"uments. Among the rest, is an official return of their "loss in the late action, by which they acknowledge nine "hundred and five, killed, wounded, and missing, without "naming the De Watteville's, whose loss is supposed to "be two or three hundred, at least."—*Letter from Major D. B. Douglass, September 9th, 1814.*

* A similar error was committed before Sebastopol.

other officers sometimes dropping in -to watch the position of the picket-guard, in the hope to catch the first flash of a musket. But it came not; and the conclusion was, at length, generally adopted that *we* must be the attacking party, if we fought at all.

After the wound of General Gaines, the command, of course, devolved upon General Ripley; but General Brown having now partially recovered from his wounds received at Niagara Falls, returned to camp, about the eleventh, and resumed the command. It was now understood, also, that large bodies of Volunteers were collected at Buffalo, about to join us; and soon, without any one having noticed the passage of boats, during the day-time, it was observed that a considerable camp of Volunteers was formed, on the lake-shore, above Towson's - battery. Some reinforcements of Regular troops also came in, from time to time. Every thing pointed towards an approaching *coup de-main ;* but when, and in what manner, was reserved to the secret councils of the Commander-in-chief, to which, in this case, few besides the Field-officers of Engineers were admitted. On the seventeenth of September, however, it was developed in the Order for the sortie. Of which I am now to speak more briefly than I could wish.

[The author was in the habit of continuing and closing his Lecture, from this point, with a series of extempore remarks, in the order of the following notes:

"1st. Plan and success of the Sortie; killed and wound-" ed: Colonel Wood.

"2nd. M Cree and Wood; General Brown's dispatches.

"3rd. Esprit de Corps, and Loyalty.

"4th. One more application: Life a warfare—A militant "or disciplinary State—Like that of a camp of In-" struction, having for its end the formation of a char-" acter—That character in a vastly higher relation "indeed may be said to be, Love of Rectitude, Fideli-" ty, Loyalty, Gen leness, Self-devotion, Implicit Obe-" dience."

It is a source of great regret that these notes were not filled out by the author's own hand. The last two, in particular, were characteristic of the man himself, and the cream of some thirty years varied experience, from the date of the campaign. Those who have heard them, will not fail to remember the remarkable clearness and vigor of the thoughts which were expressed; the strong convictions of manly duty which they carried to the heart of every hearer ; the high tone of Christian chivalry which dignified every sentence, and proved the speaker to have been, as an eloquent friend remarked, "the soldier of Cursar as " well as of his country."

For the remainder of this Lecture, the Editor must profess himself responsible. He has aimed, simply, to bring it to a proper and satisfactory conclusion ; and, in order to preserve the strict integrity of the narrative, has carefully confined himself to well-authenticated facts, with which,

however, so far as his recollection extends, the spoken narrative of the author perfectly harmonises.

Colonels Woods and M'Rea, it will be seen, are particularly noticed; for the lecturer was accustomed, not only in these lectures but, often, in the social circle, also, to acknowledge the benefits he derived from the patronage and example of both these distinguished officers. His mention of Colonel Wood, in particular, was marked with undisguised warmth and affectionate feeling. It seemed impossible for him to look back to the young days of an ardent and generous ambition, even through the long period of thirty years, without a pang of sorrow, at the recollection of the high-minded and chivalrous man, who was his friend and brother-in-arms; his companion, amidst scenes of the most soul-stirring interest; his tutor in Military Science; his mentor in the perplexities of an early and important responsibility; his guide and example, in all that was high, noble, and disinterested, in the walk and profession of a soldier.—*Rev. Malcolm Douglass, D.D.*)

It will be observed that the British batteries of which mention has been already made, were quite distinct from the British camp. The camp proper was situated, some two miles to the rear of its batteries, upon a cleared space, not far from the Niagara river, but screened by heavy forests from the risk of annoyance from the American side. For the management and protection of the batteries, however, the Infantry of the British force had been divided into three Brigades, which were appointed, alternately, to guard them against surprise. They were thus kept constantly defended by a force of from twelve to fifteen hundred men; and were strengthened, besides, along their whole line, by a complexity of defences, in front and in rear, consisting of other intrenchments, lines of brushwood, felled timber, and abattis, arranged with studied intricacy and expressly calculated to retard and confuse an assailing party. The object of *the sortie,* as General Brown concisely observes, was "to storm these "batteries, destroy their cannon, and roughly "handle the Brigade upon duty, before those "in reserve (at the British camp) could be "brought into action."*

The plan of the sortie was arranged with reference to such aims and facilities as the character of the ground afforded, in order that the attack might, so far as was practicable, have the effect of a surprise. The force which bordered upon the extreme left of our camp extended around and far beyond the enemy's

---

* For these and other items, see General Brown's Report to the Secretary of War, dated "Fort Erie. Sept. 29, "1814 ;" also General Porter's Report to the Commanding General, dated "Fort Erie, Sept. 22 1814;" also the map of the British Batteries and their defences, as sketched by D. B. Douglass, in September and October of 1814; also original letters of D. B. Douglass, dated in September and October of 1814.

batteries; and, about half way between the nearest battery and the salient point of our bastion, the upper plateau of the river was intersected by a slight ravine, which opened, indeed, in full view of the enemy, but which headed from the woods, and might, therefore, be gained, it was thought, without attracting his observation. Accordingly, on the sixteenth, fatigue-parties were sent, under the charge of able officers, to mark a road through the swampy and timbered ground; in doing which they proceeded with so much caution, that they passed the extreme right of the enemy's line, and turned upon the rear of his batteries, without discovery.

On the morning of the seventeenth, every thing appeared favorable for the meditated enterprise. The atmosphere was heavily loaded with vapors, with, now and then, a slight shower, all which was well calculated to screen our movements and to cherish our enemy's sense of security. The attack was organized to be made principally at two points. The left column, in three divisions, under General Porter, passed through the woods by the circuitous route marked out, on the preceding day, until they were within a few rods of the British right flank. The right column, commanded by General Miller, was, in the mean time, passed by small detachments, into the edge of the woods, under cover of which it marched to the head of the ravine, and, passing quietly down, took up its position nearly opposite the enemy's center. General Ripley was stationed by Fort Erie, with a column in reserve; and the artillery was put in readiness to cover the return of the troops.

About half past two in the afternoon, the action commenced with the assault of the right of the enemy's works, by our left column. The right column, under General Miller, immediately charged from the ravine; pierced the enemy's intrenchments; and succeeded in co-operating with General Porter's column. In a few minutes, they had taken possession of the block-houses; cleared the intrenchments of their defenders; captured the second and third batteries; and disabled their cannon. The British first battery held out for a short time, but was finally abandoned, when its guns also were disabled or otherwise destroyed. The whole of the enemy's reserve was, by this time, in full march for the scene of action; but the object of the sortie had been fully accomplished; and our troops retired, in good order and without molestation, to the fort.

Our losses in this affair were considerable, and were increased perhaps by the same causes—viz., the mist and rain—which had favored the attack. As, for instance, owing to the obscuri-

ty of the sun, detached parties, unacquainted with the country, moved off, at the signal for retiring, in the wrong direction, and met the enemy's approaching columns. It was in this way that we nearly lost the gallant General Miller, who was separated from his command, and, meeting the enemy's advance, saved himself only by a very speedy retreat. In this way, also, a body of fifty prisoners, who had surrendered, and were ordered to the fort, under the charge of a subaltern and fourteen volunteers, were conducted towards the British camp, and re-captured, with nearly the whole of their escort. These, with other instances of the same sort, together with the loss which necessarily accompanied the bold attack upon the batteries and breast-works, reduced our effective force upwards of five hundred men, including some highly valued officers. But unfortunate as was the battle, in this respect, it was, in itself, a most glorious achievement and very decisive for us, in the result. In one hour of close action, our two thousand Regulars and Militia destroyed the fruits of fifty days labor, and reduced the strength of the enemy, as we were informed by their own General Order, one thousand men, at the least; and gave them such an idea of Yankee courage or, as they termed it, desperation, that they broke up their encampment, on the night of the twenty first, and retired rapidly down the river.[*]

CONCLUDING NOTE.—"Amongst our losses, in "this affair," writes the lecturer, "I have the "sorrow to name our ever to be lamented and "gallant friend, Colonel Wood. He went out "with the Volunteers, and, amidst the confusion "which necessarily attends a fight in the woods, "was, somehow, separated from them. When "they returned, after the battle, he was missing. "Enquiry was made, next day, by a flag; and "we received the unwelcome intelligence that "he had been mortally wounded in the action, "and died in the British camp, the night after;" professing, it is said, the most ardent attachment to his country, and a jealous solicitude for the honor of her arms, commending her, with his last breath, to the favor and protection of the Almighty.

Thus ended his promising career. "He died, "as he had ever lived, brave, generous, and "enterprising." Modest and retiring, in his general manners; gentle as a maiden, in the society of his friends; you could scarcely recognize the same person, upon the field of battle. Wherever danger was, there was he found—fearless, self-possessed, and calm as upon parade. In action, he was like a lion. It was his

---

[*] See General Brown's Report of the Sortie; D. Douglass's correspondence; etc., etc.

peculiar good fortune to be the first in every engagement, and ever *with* the first in the estimation of his Commander. "Permit me," writes General Harrison,[*] "to recommend Captain "Wood, of the Engineers, to the President, and "to assure you that any mark of his approba- "tion bestowed upon Captain Wood would be "highly gratifying to the whole of the troops "who witnessed his arduous exertions." "From "the long illness of Captain Gratiot, of the "Corps of Engineers, the important duties of "fortifying the camp devolved on Captain Wood "of that Corps. In assigning to him the first "palm of merit, so far as relates to the transac- "tions within the works, the General is con- "vinced the same decision will be awarded by "every individual in the camp who witnessed "his indefatigable exertions, his consummate "skill in providing for the safety of every point "and in foiling every attempt of the enemy, and "his undaunted bravery in the performance of "his duty in the most exposed situations." "To "Major Wood," writes General Ripley,[†] "I feel "particularly indebted. This officer's merits "are so well known that approbation can "scarcely add to his reputation." "You "know," writes General Porter,[‡] "how exalt- "ed an opinion I have always entertained of "Lieutenant-colonel Wood, of the Engineers. "His conduct on this day" (*of the sortie*) "was "what it uniformly has been on every similar "occasion, an exhibition of military skill, acute "judgment, and heroic valor." "His name "and example," writes General Brown to the Secretary of War, "will live to guide the sol- "dier in the path of duty so long as true hero- "ism is held in estimation."[§]

McRea, too, the senior officer of the Engineer Corps, on the Niagara, must not be passed by unnoticed. Writing of the Battle of Lundy's-lane,[|] General Brown remarks: "The Engin- "eers, Majors McRea and Wood, were greatly "distinguished on this day, and their high "military talents exerted with great effect; "they were much under my eye and near my "person, and to their assistance a great deal is "fairly to be ascribed. I most earnestly recom- "mend them as worthy of the highest trust "and confidence." "Major, or as he is now, "Colonel, McRea's industry and talents are the

"admiration of the whole army." [*] After the sortie, General Brown thus writes,[†] "Lieutenant- "colonels McRea and Woo l having rendered "to this army services the most important, I "must seize the opportunity of again mention- "ing them, particularly. On every trying occa- "sion, I have reaped much benefit from their "sound and excellent advice. No two officers "of their grade could have contribute l more "to the safety and honor of this army, • • • "McRea still lives to enjoy the approbation of "every virtuous and generous mind, and to re- "ceive the reward due to his services and high "military talents." But that reward, it seems, was never forthcoming. With science and military talent of the very highest eminence, and a genius for command able to direct the operations of the largest army which could be brought into the field, he, together with the other long-distinguished and able officers of the Engineer Corps, was passed by for a foreign- er. Colonel McRea, himself, aided and contrib- uted to the success of the negotiations which brought General Bernard to this country; and, having done all that he could do, in the faith- ful discharge of this duty, he resigned his commission, with a wounded heart, and retired from the service to private life. He died, in 1832, of the cholera.

The lecturer's own words, on the first of October, 1814, will conclude the narrative of his share in the events of this Campaign: "Now that the British force have retired, my "time is spent very differently from what it was "a few weeks since. The large details of men "have ceased, in a great measure; and, instead "of being incessantly engaged in the engineer "work or the batteries and bastion, I take out "a squad of Bombardiers and spend my time, "very quietly, in measuring the principal lines "about the camp and the adjacent country. "This, always a favorite employment with me, "would be still more delightful if I had any "instruments to work with; but, the difficulty "is, that I have no means, except of my own "invention, for measuring either a line or an "angle; and it is necessary to go over some of "my work, two or three times, in different "ways, to prove its correctness or detect any "error which might occur. For my lines, I use "an old cord with half a dozen knots in it, to "which I am obliged to apply a ten-foot pole, "every five minutes, to correct its variations. "As for my angles, I have divers ways and some "very wonderful ones, too, of ascertaining "them."

---

[*] General Harrison to the Secretary of War, "Fort "Meigs, May 9, 1813:" General Harrison's "General Or- "ders," Fort Meigs, May 9, 1813. •

[†] To the Commanding General, "Fort Erie, August 17, "1814."

[‡] To the Commanding General, "Fort Erie, September "20, 1814."

[§] The monument, at West Point, erected to his memory by General Brown.

[|] To the Secretary of War, "Buffalo, August, 1814."

[*] D. B. Douglass, "Fort Erie, September 9, 1814."

[†] To the Secretary of War, "Fort Erie, September 20, "1814."

October 18th, 1814. " From the time I
" wrote my last letter, I continued to employ
" myself, as there stated, but I had hardly com-
" pleted my rough sketches of the ground, un-
" til loss of appetite and health compelled me
" to be confined to my quarters. The extreme-
" ly unhealthy nature of under-ground quarters,
" such as mine, rendered them very unfit for
" the residence of a healthy man, and much
" more so for one in my situation. I became
" weaker and weaker, every day, while I remain-
" ed in them, until Colonel McRea procured an
" order for me to be removed to Williamsville,
" on the American side."

The exposures, fatigues, privations, and
anxieties, of this eventful Campaign had proved
too much for him. He languished for many
days, under a bilious fever, from which, however, by the blessing of God, his naturally
elastic and vigorous constitution gradually
recovered.

[To be Continued.]

III.—*THE WESTERN STATES OF THE GREAT VALLEY; AND THE CAUSE OF THEIR PROSPERITY, HISTORICALLY CONSIDERED.*—Concluded from Page 89.

By Joseph F. Tuttle, D.D., President of
Wabash-college, Indiana.

" *July 18th.*—Paid my respects, this morning,
" to the President of Congress, Gen. St. Clair.
" Called on a number of my friends. Attended
" at the City Hall, on members of Congress and
" their Committee. We renewed our negotia-
" tions. Dined with Capt. Hammond, in com-
" pany with a young Irish nobleman and Mr.
" Hillegass, Treasurer of the United States, and
" some other company. Drank tea and spent
" the evening at Sir John Temple's. This day
" is Commencement, at Cambridge, which Major
" Sargent, Gen. Webb, and a few others call
" ed to mind; and we celebrated it, at eleven
" o'clock, at General Webb's, with a bottle or
" two of wine and some good old Cheshire
" cheese. We conclude they must have had a
" fine Commencement, if the atmosphere at Cam
" bridge has been as fine and cool as our's, in
" New York.
. " *July 19.*—Called on members of Congress
" very early this morning. Was furnished with
" the Ordinance establishing a Government in
" the Western Federal Territory. *It is, in a*
" *degree, new modelled. The amendments I pro-*
" *posed have all been made, except one; and that*
" *is better qualified.* It was that we should not
" be subject to Continental taxation, until we

" were entitled to a full representation in Con-
" gress. This could not be fully obtained, for
" it was considered, in Congress, as offering a
" premium to emigrants. They have granted us
" representation, with the right of debating, but
" not of voting, upon our being first subject to
" taxation. As there are a number, in Congress,
" decidedly opposed to my terms of negotia-
" tions, and some to any contract, I wish now to
" ascertain the number for and against; and
" who they are; and must then, if possible,
" bring the opponents over. This I have men-
" tioned to Col. Duer, who has promised to assist
" me. Grayson, R. H. Lee, and Carrington are,
" certainly, my warm advocates. Holton, I
" think, may be trusted. *Dane must be careful-*
" *ly watched, notwithstanding his professions.*
" Clarke, Bingham, Yates, Kearney, and Few
" are troublesome fellows. They must be at-
" tacked by my friends, at their lodgings. If
" they can be brought over, I shall succeed; if
" not, my business is at an end. Attended the
" Committee, this morning. They are determin-
" ed to make a report, to-day, and try the spirit
" of Congress. Dined with Gen. Knox—about
" forty gentlemen, officers of the late Continen-
" tal Army, and among them Baron Steuben.
" Gen. Knox gave us an entertainment in the
" style of a prince. I had the honor of being
" seated next to the Baron, who is a hearty, so-
" ciable, old fellow. He was dressed in his
" military uniform, and with the ensigns of no-
" bility—the Star and Garter. Every gentlemen,
" at table, was of the Cincinnati, except myself,
" and wore their appropriate badges. Spent
" the evening at Dr. Holton's, with Col. Duer
" and several members of Congress, who in-
" formed me an Ordinance was passed, in con-
" sequence of my petition; but, by their ac-
" count of it, it will answer no purpose.
" *July 20.*—This morning, the Secretary of
" Congress furnished me with the Ordinance of
" yesterday, which states the conditions of a
" contract, but on terms to which I shall by no
" means accede. Informed the Committee of
" Congress that I could not contract on the terms
" proposed. Should prefer purchasing lands of
" some of the States, who would give incom-
" parably better terms, and therefore proposed
" to leave the city, immediately. They appear-
" ed to be very sorry no better terms were offer-
" ed, and insisted on my not thinking of leaving
" Congress, until another attempt was made. I
" told them I saw no prospect of a contract;
" and wished to spend no more time and money
" in a business so unpromising. They assured
" me I had many friends in Congress, who
" would make every exertion in my favor; that
" it was an object of great magnitude; and I
" must not expect to accomplish it, in less than

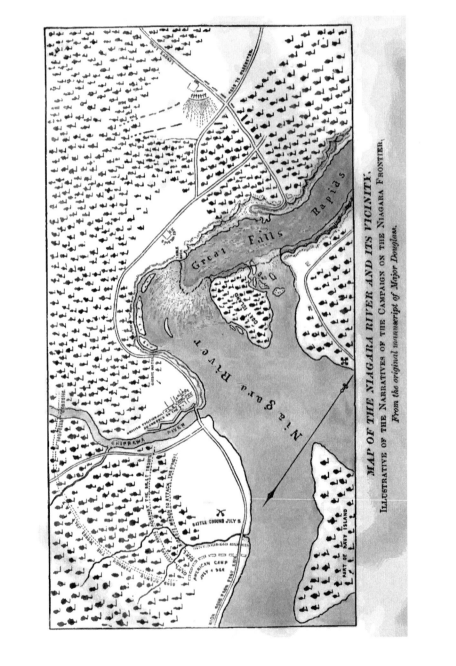

MAP OF THE NIAGARA RIVER AND ITS VICINITY,

ILLUSTRATIVE OF THE NARRATIVES OF THE CAMPAIGN ON THE NIAGARA FRONTIER,

From the original manuscript of Major Douglass.

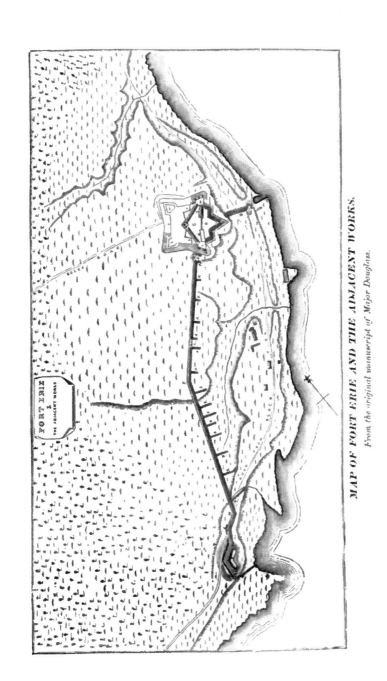

MAP OF FORT ERIE AND THE ADJACENT WORKS.

From the original manuscript of Major Douglass.

mile above town 5 marched 6 miles in direction of shepards town & c. 6 marched 4 miles & back on Picket 1½ mile of the E. heard their drums & band Playing at Harpers ferry sunday *7 still on P. lad for the E.

12 oc. Left Dufield Depot & marched to ee town 8 Remained 9 Remained 10 marched to winches & held our horses all night & in the morning 11 commenst scrimishing freed artilery a few rounds & marched the X Reds above mill Bur & had a hard scrimmish tight & marched to this River be low Straws Burg 12 marched 8 miles above front Royal & C 13 back to front Royal on P. Sunday 14th Reinforced by fitzuel Lee by a larg force 15 Returned to Camp 16 moved with in 4 miles of F Royal & C. fitzuel Lee had a fight with Sabours & killed & wonded 80 of the E. 17 marched 4 miles below front Royel & was orderd back marcked 10 miles & C. 18 marched threw Lieuray & on to Pnew marke & camped 19 Remained 20 Started hom 21 got home Remained until the 25 Started to camp got to Samuel Snars 26 to Broos town met a variety of wonde soldiers on their way to winchester from a fight they had the night before at Lee town 27 found the command below Lee town & moved above & c 28 moved up to Smith field & grazed by the bridel untill 1 oc. the Pick ware drawn in to Smith field & a heavy Skrimishing & artilery duel kept up untill night, morning of the 29 very Earley in the mornin the E Pursuied us in the Direc of Binkers hill we took a Stan & drove them Back 30 all quiet weare on Picket awaiting to heare the orders of the 10 oc. we ware orderd down to a Pecken & Remained all day Saw some yankeys & was Releived by the 62 & fell Back 1 mile morning 31 quite Early heard fireing on the martings Burg Rode it turned out to be a small scouting Party 12 oc. Started up the valey got 5 miles a bove Bunkes Hill & about faced & back to fore said camp

thurs day Sept 1th to Stephensons Depoe 2 marched 1 s. 6 & grazed & back to camp thare was a considerable Cavelry fite below Bunker hill Ourmen fell back) 3 marched down to the Jarits town Rode on reaching the fore Said Rode we found a heavy cavelry schrimushing going on our squadring was sent out on the Jarrits town Rode on Picket soon we was orderd to fall Back Rhapidly to Bunkers hill & as we got thar we found the valey over spread with troops & in a heavy ingagement a fighting we Pitched in & helped them & the infantry & artilery came up and the fight silenced here we went in the direction of Smith field on Picket & about 5 oc thar was a heavy ingagement commenst about Bery vill & laste untill some time after night we Remained all night) morning of the 4 Sunday Still heard cannon in the direction) or left of Bery vill & some Skrimish Below Bunker hill 9 oc. we ware

orderd to fall back. the yankeys pushed us hard for 6 miles skrimishing all the way we took a stan 6 miles below Winchester & held our Position all night morning of 5th commenst sk. by day Light & heard small armes in the direction of Bery vill about 4 oc the E advanced on us Rhapidly we stood them a hard fight I got shot threw the Pants several slightly wonded 1 Private & c onel kiled & sevial horses killed & wonded we drove them back 5 miles kill 7 & went on Picket) 6 skrimished a little all day & camped on the same ground 7 about 4 oc the E advanced a small skrimish line & drove our Pickets in we advanced on them & drove them back to Bunkers hill & fell back to fore Said Camp & Remained all night we got 2 horses wonded & killed 1 for them thursday morning sep 8th still skrimishing in the Evening went on P. 9 moved down 2 miles the E. has fell back. 10 marched down below Bunkers hill the Infantry fowling coommenst skrimishing & drove the E below martains Burg driving the E all the way & fell back to Bunker hill or East of thare & camp 11 marched 2 miles above B. H. & graized & went on P. 12 Relieved & bac k to fore said Camp abov B.s H. 13 Heard heavy Cannonddieng to the right of Smith field 2 oc mounted & went down to wards B.s h & had a hard skrimish fight with 3 hnn yankeys drove them back kill a few we got one w. & back to camp

wednsday sep 14th went on P on the Smith field Road 15 all quiet at 3 oC Relieved & Back to camp 16 Remained 17 went on P. sunday 18th the yankey Drum & Rebel Drum is sonding around what the move is I cannot tell Monday morning 19th by day Ligt I heard a heavy engagement commense to the left of winchest 10 oc skrimishing commenst at Bunkers hill we fell back fighting at intervels all the way to winchester some times the E. charging us & some times we chargeing them back we lost 2 men kill 1 Lieut wonded in Co B the Balance suferd in like manner) we assended the hights at winchester & looked over the wide extended Plains of winchester & as far as my eyes could see I beheld a mighty concorse of yankeys & Rebels ingagued in the most heart Rending conflict which was to hard for us we fell Back to cedar creek & fed & lay in the road untill morning of the 20 then moved to fishers hill & thar took a Position & whilest hearing the Bands Play I was mad to inquire whare are the many dead & wonded that Listend at this sweet music a few evenings ago the E. is in hearing distance now how soon we will have to meet them again I cant tell about midnight we marchd out on the Left of our line & fortifed & at day light of the 21 skrimishing commeneg all a long our lines We are Lying awaiting to Be atackted * *

III.—*REMINISCENCES OF THE CAM-*
PAIGN OF 1814, ON THE NIAGARA
FRONTIER. --CONCLUDED FROM PAGE 142.

FROM THE PAPERS OF THE LATE DAVID B. DOUG-
LASS, LL.D., FORMERLY CAPTAIN OF ENGIN-
EERS, U. S. A.; COMMUNICATED BY HIS CHIL-
DREN, FOR PUBLICATION IN THE HISTORICAL
MAGAZINE.

1.—DESCRIPTION OF FORT ERIE.

*[From a letter written by Lieutenant Douglass to
Andrew Ellicot, August, 1814.*]*

The small Battery (marked A) on the extreme right was called the Douglass Battery. It
was situated on a ridge of ground, about nine
feet higher than the water of the lake, and
immediately in rear of an excavation which
had been made for the purpose of quarrying
the lime-stone. Its parapet was sixteen feet
thick, at top; between eight and nine feet high,
on the outside; and very much sloped. Its
platform was *en barbette*, and estimated at about
seventeen feet square.†

The space between the Douglass Battery and
the lake was undefended by any work. A six-
pounder, however, (marked a) belonging to my
command, was commonly placed in a situation
to defend the approach to it; and, on the morning of the fifteenth of August, it was further
defended by a detachment of General Porter's
Volunteers (marked b). The epaulment (marked
B) on the left of the Douglass Battery, was that
which covered the Ninth Regiment. It was

about eighteen feet in thickness, and from six
and a half to seven feet in height, with both
faces nearly perpendicular. Its ditch was of
different dimensions, at different parts, but generally of small account. The space between
the left of this epaulment and the nearest part
of Fort Erie, was closed only by a slight
abattis.

Immediately to the left of the Douglass Battery, the ground descended a few feet; but, towards the extremity of the line described, it rose
again; forming, a little further on, an elevation
of about seventeen or eighteen feet above the
level of the lake. Upon this elevation stood old
Fort Erie. The out-line of Fort Erie, as it was
originally projected, is denoted by the line *c. d.
e. f. g. h. i. j. k.;* but of this no part had been
wrought upon, to any extent, except the two Bastions (L and M), the mess-houses (N and O), and
the curtain (k and e). These, with the other works
which go to enclose the areas C and D, constituted, on the fifteenth of August, the whole of
what was properly called Fort Erie.

The extreme faces of the salient Bastion (M)
were constructed partly of stone and partly of
earth. That on the South, was a simple stone-
wall, about three feet thick. The other had an
escarpe of stone, surmounted by an earthen parapet. The height of the former was not more
than ten or eleven feet; but the latter, ditched
as it was, and surmounted with earth, had a
height of at least twenty-two or twenty-three
feet, including merlons of four feet. The
counter-scarpe of the ditch was steep but not
regularly formed. The number of embrasures
and shape of the platform was as represented in
the drawing—the height of the latter being
about five feet above the level of the Fort.

The other Bastion (L) was nearly the same as
the one just described, except in the number of
its embrasures and shape of its platform.

The Mess-houses (N and O), were built in the
prolongation of the South faces of the Bastions
(L and M). They were ninety-three feet long
and two stories high, built of stone, forming
one wall with the revetments to which they
joined. In the second story, they had each a
line of loop-holes, on their water-fronts, and on

---

* Some of the references—mainly those in *small* letters
—cannot be found on the map which faces this page.
The small scale on which it was necessarily drawn, compelled the engraver to omit some of the references which
appear on the large map—which is many times larger than
this—in order to prevent the whole from being unintelligi-
ble by being too much crowded.—EDITOR.

† The following remarks and observations may prove
useful to the unmilitary reader: " A permanent fortifica-
"tion, in its most simple form, consists of a mound of
"earth, termed *the Rampart*, which encloses the space
"fortified; a *Parapet*, surrounding the Rampart and cov-
"ering the men and guns from the enemy's projectiles; a
"*Scarp-wall*, which sustains the pressure of the earth of
"the Rampart and Parapet, and presents an insurmount-
"able obstacle to an assault by storm; a wide and deep
"*Ditch*, which prevents the enemy from approaching near
"the body of the place; a *Counter Scarp-wall*, which
"sustains the earth on the exterior of the Ditch; and a
"mound of earth, called a *Glacis*, thrown up a few yards
"in front of the Ditch, for the purpose of covering the
"Scarp of the main work."—Halleck's *Military Art and
Science.*

Openings cut in the Parapet, and through which the
guns are pointed, are called *Embrasures.* The mass of

earth between the Embrasures is called a *Merlon*, and pro-
tects the men from the enemy's fire. When the Parapet
is not pierced with Embrasures, the guns are pointed over
it; and are then said to be *en-barbett.* In this position,
though more exposed, they command a much wider field
than when in *embrasure.* The Epaulment is an earthen
breastwork.

The works at Fort Erie, being partly temporary and
partly permanent fortifications, and for the most part very
hastily thrown up, the Rampart and Parapet are called,
indifferently, " the Parapet," in this description.

the short flanks at k and c. The one marked n was entirely dismantled, as represented in the drawing ; and the other had been somewhat injured, at the Northwest end, by the enemy's shot. By the position of these Block-houses, the gorges of their respective Bastions were reduced to about seven feet in width. The Curtain (k. and c.) was, by estimation, fifteen feet high and three feet thick, having the gateway in the center.

The works, thus far described, were made into a complete enclosure by means of the temporary salient Curtain (q. r. p.), both branches of which consisted of a series of banquettes, and a parapet equal in height to those of the Bastions (L and M). On the fifteenth of August, however, they were imperfectly joined to the little Battery (r), particularly on the South-west side. The Battery (r) was very small, having a platform scarcely twelve feet square. I am unable to say whether it may not have been en-barbett on the fifteenth of August. Its height was the same as the branches just described, and, like them, it had a ditch, three or four feet deep and about eight feet in breadth. While Fort Erie was yet in the hands of the enemy, the purposes of this curtain had been answered by a line of pickets (S.R.T.), most of which were still standing, on the fifteenth of August—they were about eleven feet high. The work inclosing the area (marked D) was an out-work of earth, constructed for the security of the gateway of the Fort. Its parapet is estimated to have been   feet thick at the top and about six and a half feet high from the berm; and its ditch five feet deep and   feet wide. Its entrance was near the wall of the Fort, on the North-east side, and in the salient angle (marked u,) was a platform for one gun, en-barbett. A considerable quantity of earth had been thrown up at the Bastions (V and W)—the latter of which had an escarpe of masonry. The little Battery (E), on the glacis of the Bastion (L), was the one which was occupied, on the fifteenth, by Captain Fanning. I think it had merlons at the time; but I cannot say with certainty. From the left of Fanning's Battery, the line of defence extended, as in the drawing,   yards to the salient angle (F). From thence it ran in a direction nearly South (yards,) to the recentering angle (H); thence to I (yards) and lastly (yards) to Towson's Battery. K. It consisted of a Breastwork; with banquettes and a ditch ; but as it was built in haste, by the Regiments who respectively occupied it, no particular care was taken to have them of any uniform dimensions. The height of the Breastwork was generally about six and a half or seven feet; that in thickness it varied from five to sixteen feet. The Ditch was from six to ten feet wide and, generally, about three

or four feet deep. The interior of the Breastwork was deflladed by Traverses (X. X. X.), at right angles. The position of Captain Biddle's Company of Artillery is marked G. The attention of the Engineers being, of course, principally directed to the flanks, I am unable to say whether the whole of the line, just described, was completed by the fifteenth of August or not. The first part, as far as the salient angle F, I think was so; but the second part, between F and H, may not have been quite as much so as I have represented it. The ground, however, in this quarter, was, for the most part, low and marshy ; and the line which, on this account, was difficult of access, had been rendered still more so by felling the trees in front.

Towson's Battery (marked K) terminated our defences, on the left. It consisted of two faces meeting in a very obtuse salient angle—that on the right, calculated for the support of Fort Erie and the intermediate line ; the other for the particular defence of this flank. It was built on a hillock of sand, which, being easily thrown up, was quickly formed into a Rampart, upwards of twenty feet high, the platform of which was nearly thirty feet above the level of the lake. This height enabled it to overlook the rising ground (marked L) beyond it. The length of its faces was calculated to admit of mounting at least three guns on each ; that on the right, however, was not completed, and the other had, I think, low merlons, at the time of the action. Towson's Battery and the Bastions V and W were, wrought exclusively by general fatigues, under the immediate direction of the officers of Engineers.

The space between Towson's Battery and the lake is closed, in the drawing, with an abattis, which extended around the front of Towson's Battery. The encampment of Colonel Wood's Corps, consisting of the Twenty-first Infantry, is marked Y.

2.—LETTER FROM PROFESSOR W. D. WILSON.

[From The Buffalo Daily Courier, Buffalo, October 28, 1853.]

MR. SEAVER,

DEAR SIR : Sometime in the Fall of 1850, I had the pleasure of reading the History of the Niagara Campaign, during the war with England, written by the late Major Douglass. I hope and trust that this history will soon be given to the public, with a biographical notice worthy of one who deserved so much of his country. In this history, the Major has spoken of the explosion of the Magazine, during the sortie upon Fort Erie, in August, 1814, upon which the result of the attack depended—and, in a great measure, the termination of the war also—as a casualty, which occurred from some unknown cause.

I remembered, in reading the Major's graphic description, the account which I had heard, some years before, from a Mr. Daw, who was present on the occasion. I thereupon wrote to an old friend, residing in the same village as Mr. Daw, asking him to see Daw and get from him a statement of his recollection of the manner of the explosion. Doctor Moor, the friend to whom I wrote, happened to be, at the time, Notary Public, and, very kindly, called upon Mr. Daw; and, in a few days, sent me the following affidavit:

"I, James Daw, of Littleton, New Hamp-"shire, depose and say, that I am fifty-eight "years old.

"I enlisted into the Army of the United "States, in April, 1814, and was enrolled in the "Company of Daniel Ketchum.

"I was within the Bastion of Fort Erie when "the Magazine exploded, in August, 1814, while "the British Army was attempting to re-take "the Fort.

"It was known to me and others, some days "before that event, that preparations had been "made to fire the Magazine, in case the Fort "could not otherwise be defended.

"We were attacked before the arrangement "was completed. The design was to have "placed in the Magazine, a keg of powder, in "connection with about twenty more already "placed there, and to connect, with this, a large "piece of port-fire, to enable the person who ap-"plied the match, to do it with safety to him-"self. Instead of this, there was only a train "of powder strown on the ground to the Maga-"zine.

"A Lieutenant of Bombardiers volunteered "to fire it. He was seen to apply the match "more than once, as the whole train of powder "did not burn on the first application, and he "was obliged to advance so near that he was "killed by the explosion.

"The subject was often talked of among us; "and the act of the officer who applied the "match was always regarded as one of extra-"ordinary daring. I never heard any one name "the explosion of the Magazine as an accident.
"JAMES DAW,
"Twenty-fifth Reg."

Doctor Moor then officially certifies that James Daw, the signer of the above, personally appeared, and made solemn oath that the foregoing affidavit was true, before him, as Notary Public.

This affidavit was sworn to, at Littleton, New Hampshire, on the twenty-second of October, 1853.

This certainly is an important document, and, if true, the noble daring and self-sacrifice of the Lieutenant of Bombardiers should be known and rewarded with the gratitude of his countrymen, which is due to them.

Doctor Moor adds that he believes Mr. Daw to be "a man whose statements may be fully "relied upon." I can add that I knew Mr. Daw, some twelve or fifteen years ago, and regarded him, and think he was generally regarded, as a man of veracity. I never heard his veracity called in question.

I send this document to you, believing you will be glad to insert it in the *Courier*. Buffalo being so near the scene of the occurrence to which it relates, I have supposed that its publication there would be more likely to revive and call forth the recollection of some other person, on a subject of so much national interest, than in any other place.

I am, Very Truly, Yours,
W. D. WILSON.
GENEVA, N. Y., Oct. 26, 1853.

3.—ANSWER TO PROFESSOR W. D. WILSON'S LETTER, BY REV. MALCOLM DOUGLASS, A SON OF MAJOR D. B. DOUGLASS.

[*From* The Buffalo Daily Courier, *Buffalo, November 14, 1853.*]

ALBION, Nov. 7, 1853.
MR. SEAVER:

I have been favored, by a friend, with a copy of the *Buffalo Courier*, for the twenty-eighth of October. It contains, I perceive, a communication calling public attention to the stirring event at Fort Erie, during the siege in the Campaign of 1814, and, especially, to the explosion in the contested Bastion of the Fort, during the night-attack of the British force. The question as to the *cause* of this explosion is proposed; and the testimony of Mr. James Daw—at the time, a soldier in the Twenty-fifth Regiment—is furnished, to the effect that it was the result, not of accident, but of a pre-concerted plan. May I crave the insertion of a few words upon this subject?

I have, at hand, the manuscript Lectures of Major Douglass, on the Niagara Campaign, referred to by your correspondent; and I take leave to quote the passage which bears upon the point in question: "It is not difficult to "account for the cause of the explosion of the "Bastion. The Magazine was under the Plat-"form and quite open. In the haste and ardor "with which the guns were served, during the "action, and in the confusion of the *melee*, some "cartridges were, doubtless, broken and the "powder strewed around, forming a train, or "succession of trains, connecting with the

"Magazine, which a burning wad or the dis-
"charge of a musket might easily ignite." It
will be observed that this conjecture does not
agree with the statement of Mr. Daw; and I
still think, with such attention as I have been
able to give the question and without impugning the veracity of Mr. Daw, that the above
statement is the more accurate and reasonable
of the two. I may observe, by the way, that
this was a subject to which Major Douglass had
devoted a great deal of attention: for he was
not unaware that the question was debated. I
distinctly remember having heard him say that,
at various times since the Campaign, he had
compared notes with his brother officers, who
were also eye-witnesses of the explosion, and
the impression which he formed, at the period
of the siege, were only more and more *confirm-
ed*, viz.: that it was purely accidental.

I have regarded Mr. Daw's statement as inac-
curate in its principal points. His first statement is as follows: "It was known to me and
"others, some days before that event, that
"preparations had been made to fire the Maga-
"zine in case the Fort could not otherwise be
"defended. We were attacked before the ar-
"rangement was completed," etc. Now the
public and private statements of Major Douglass assure us that no such arrangement was
known to the Engineer officers, who are always
entrusted with the superintendence of affairs of
this kind, in the defence of fortified camps.
No such arrangements were known to the General commanding, who, in his Report to the
Secretary of War, acknowledges the Chief Engineer's correct and seasonable suggestions to
regain the Bastion; and, while giving some of
the details of this very attempt to regain it,
he adds: "at this moment, every operation
"was arrested by the explosion of some cart-
"ridges, deposited at the end of the stone-
"building, adjoining the contested Bastion.
"The explosion was tremendous—it was de-
"cisive; the Bastion was restored." So far,
then, as the officers are concerned, the occurrence does not seem to be pre-concerted;
and, as Mr. Daw evidently does not regard it
as the secret work of private soldiers, it would
seem not unlikely that he and his fellow-soldiers
misinterpreted some directions and arrangements in the construction of the Bastion, which
was unfinished, up to the time of the attack.

Mr. Daw further states that "a Lieutenant of
"Bombardiers volunteered to fire it. He was
"seen to apply the match, more than once, as
"the whole train of powder did not burn on
"the first application, and he was obliged to
"advance so near, that he was killed by the
"explosion. The subject was often talked of
"among us, and the act of the officer, who ap-

"plied the match, was always regarded as one
"of most extraordinary daring." Now Major
Douglass was the only Lieutenant of Bombardiers in the action. The Company of Bombardiers and Sappers and Miners was under his
especial command, as an Engineer officer. His
Junior, Lieutenant Story, was on duty on the
American side. Captain Williams and Lieutenant McDonough, both of the Artillery, are
the *only* officers mentioned in General Gaines's
Report as killed, and they were known to have
been killed before the Bastion was yielded to
the enemy. Is it not likely, then, that Mr.
Daw's statement, on this point, is one of those
mistaken rumors which would naturally cir-
culate among the private soldiers, after the
battle, and which, at such a time, can easily
gain currency with many, upon very insufficient evidence? And does it not appear that,
until more decisive evidence, to the contrary,
is advanced, the statement in the Niagara Lectures has, by far, the greatest probability in its
favor? My own opinion is, decidedly, in the
affirmative.

Major Douglass's account of the explosion
may be interesting to your readers. It is as
follows: "The Bastion, itself, was still in the
"possession of the enemy; but it was under-
"stood that they were not only unable to pene-
"trate further, but that they had been terribly
"cut up by the fires from the Block-house and
"from other adjacent parts of the Fort and
"outworks. Several charges had been made
"upon them, but, owing to the narrowness of
"the passage and the height of the platform,
"they had, as yet, been unsuccessful. Another
"party, however, it was said, of picked men,
"was now just organized, with the hope of a
"better result. To this enterprise, then, the
"only thing now remaining to complete the
"repulse of the enemy, the attention of every
"beholder was most anxiously bent. The fir-
"ing within the Fort had already begun to
"slacken, as if to give place to the charging
"party; the next moment was to give us the
"clang of weapons in deadly strife. But, sud-
"denly, every sound was hushed by the sense of
"an unnatural tremor beneath our feet, like the
"first heave of an earthquake; and, almost at
"the same instant, the centre of the Bastion
"burst up with a terrific explosion; and a jet
"flame, mingled with fragments of timber,
"earth, stone, and the bodies of men, rose to
"the height of one or two hundred feet in the
"air, and fell, in a shower of ruins, to a great
"distance, all around." *   *   *   *

In another place, he thus remarks: "As to
"its effect in deciding the contest, it was very
"small, if anything. The British General
"found it very convenient to assign the explo-

"sion as the chief cause of the failure of the
"enterprise. But he had been completely re-
"pulsed, with dreadful carnage, at all points,
"*before* the explosion—the British troops in the
"Bastion were unable to advance; their com-
"mander was killed; their numbers were mo-
"mentarily thinned by our fires; and so com-
"pletely were they cut up and disabled, that of
"those removed from the ruins of the Bastion,
"but a very few were free from severe gun-
"shot wounds. Indeed, had the explosion
"been a few minutes later, the whole of their
"Reserve would, probably, have been inter-
"cepted and cut off, by a strong detachment,
"which was in motion for that purpose."

I have, I fear, taken up your attention with
a tedious letter; but it seemed called for by
the statements which were made through the
means of your esteemed correspondent. Perhaps the Memoir and the Lectures may yet be
forthcoming, and at no distant date. And I
may here say, that any well-authenticated data
which may be furnished me—letters, memoranda, notes, and the like—bearing upon any or
all of the events of the Niagara Campaign, will
be thankfully received and acknowledged.

I am, with great regard,

Yours, Very Truly,

MALCOLM DOUGLASS.

**4.—ANSWER TO PROFESSOR WILSON'S LETTER,
BY EBENEZER MIX, ESQR., OF BATAVIA, NEW
YORK.**

[*From* The Spirit of the Times, *Batavia, N. Y.,
November 15, 1853.*]

BATAVIA, Nov. 15, 1853.

MR. HURLEY:

I observe, in the *Buffalo Courier* of the
twenty-eighth ultimo, a communication from
Professor Wilson of Geneva, with the accompanying affidavit of Mr. Daw, the introduction
to which contains a request, that "old inhabi-
"tants" will give their recollections on the
subject to the public, and, as no one will dispute my being one of the "Old Inhabitants,"
and, believing myself somewhat qualified for
the task, I cheerfully comply with the request.

Far from attempting to impugn the veracity
or question the integrity or respectability of
any person connected with that communication,
I must entirely disagree with it, in relation to
the main incidents therein stated, on which
any doubts can arise. The discrepancy between
our statements is easily accounted for, as Mr.
Wilson, I presume, is not a military man, and
would not claim to be familiar with the locali-
ties of "Old Fort Erie," or the exact application of military parlance; while Mr. Daw, according to his own account, was, at that time,
a mere youth, of the age of twenty years, and

a new recruit in the service. He, too, as appears
from his statement, has lost his recollection of
military terms and phrases, or he would not
have said, in the commencement, that he "was
"within the Bastion, when the Magazine ex-
"ploded"—had he been within the Bastion,
at the time the basket of cartridges exploded,
he would not, probably, at any time since,
have been in Littleton, New Hampshire, to
have told the tale; as every man, whether
British or American, in or near the Bastion, on
or about the level of its plank-platform, at
that time, and many below, were either killed
or so severely wounded and horribly mangled,
that death was the result. Mr. Daw undoubtedly meant, that he was within the Fort—the
military encampment, called Fort Erie—at the
time of the explosion, and would so amend
his statement, if now revised by him, not that
he, a young Infantry private and a new recruit,
was, at that time, within the works of the
"Old Fort," occupied, exclusively, by Officers,
Artillerymen, and Bombardiers, and visited
only by such persons as the officers saw fit to
invite and admit. Mr. Daw was, at that time,
undoubtedly where his duty called him, and
where, had he been otherwise inclined, his officers would have compelled him to be, on
parade in the plaza, in front of the space, between the second and third traverses, counting
from the "Old Fort," in which, if I mistake
not, his Regiment, the Twenty-fifth, was encamped, there ready to march, or stand and
combat the enemy, as commanded by his officers, for it will be understood, that the Infantry,
generally, were not called into actual conflict
with the enemy, that night, but were mustered
and stood at their respective posts, ready to
obey orders, although the Twenty-first and part
of the Twenty-third Regiments did great execution in defending our southern or left extremity, near which they were encamped, as
did the Heavy Artillery and Light Corps, in
defending the northern or right flank of our
encampment.

It is said that he who demolishes an edifice,
let it be ever so mis-shapen and incommodious,
without erecting another, has been guilty of
an injury to the public weal. To avoid such
an imputation, I will give a succinct account
of the assault on Fort Erie, by the British, in
August, 1814, which I believe to be true, and
know that it was uncontradicted, in any of its
essential points, at the time it transpired, by
any intelligent person who pretended to be acquainted with its details.

That the reader may the better understand
the following statement, I will give an extract
from Turner's *Pioneer History of the Holland
Purchase of Western New York*, etc., being a

description of Fort Erie, as it existed in 1814—as its works are now almost entirely demolished, scarcely leaving a trace to designate its former location:

"Fort Erie, or rather the encampment call-"ed by that name, lying at the outlet of Lake "Erie into Niagara-river, on the Canada side, "was, at that time, composed of old 'Old Fort "'Erie,' consisting of two large stone mess-"houses and one Bastion, mounted with can-"non, situated near the margin of Niagara-"river, and a high artificial mound, transformed "from Snake-hill, about one hundred and fifty "yards southerly of the 'Old Fort.' This redoubt "was connected with the 'Old Fort' by a par-"apet of earth, thrown up between them, with "a western angle; from this Parapet, traverses "extending into the encampment.† The open "esplanade, on the West and North of our "works, was but from sixty to eighty rods "wide, where it terminated in a dense forest, "standing on a marshy or swamp bottom. Be-"tween this lengthy parapet and the shores of "the Niagara-river and Lake Erie, mostly be-"tween the traverses, was the encampment of "our regular soldiers."

On the third of July, 1814, the American Army took undisputed possession of Fort Erie; and all its forces, on the Niagara frontier, concentrated within it and on the adjacent grounds, soon after the battles of Chippewa and Lundy's-lane. In the latter part of July, the British troops, on the Niagara frontier, amounting to about five thousand, four hundred of which were veterans of European peninsular fame, under the command of Major-general Drummond, encamped on a farm, a mile and a half northwesterly of the Fort, making apparent demonstrations to invest it for a siege, but privately preparing to take it by storm, or assault. For this purpose, the assaulting forces were divided into three Divisions, one of which was to commence the attack on Towson's Battery, the entrance South of the American encampment; another Division, under the immediate command of Colonel (not General) Drummond, was to attack the only Bastion in the "Old Fort;" while the third and largest Division, was to silence Douglass's Battery, a small work near the Niagara-river, and march into the American encampment, along the Ni-

* This description, as well as the account of the sortie, contained in that volumn, was written by myself, and mostly from memoranda taken at the time of the events.
†₂The transformation of Snake-hill into "Towson's Bat-"tery." the erection of "Douglass's Battery," and all the parapets, not included in the "Old Fort," was the work of the Americans, after they took possession, on the third of July.

agara shore. The night of the fourteenth of August, which was a dark night, was selected for the enterprise, and midnight the hour.

Agreeably with this arrangement, the attack was made on Towson's Battery, but without the least success. So conspicuous was this impediment, that the British soldiers called it "The "Light House." This Division then undertook to turn our works, by fording the margin of the lake; but they were so unsparingly cut down, by the sharp-shooters of the Twenty-first and Twenty-third Regiments, as soon as they rounded the abbatis, that they were glad to desist, and retreated in disorder. Drummond, at the head of his Division, scaled the outer walls, or rather embankment—twelve or fifteen feet in perpendicular height—of the only Bastion in the "Old Fort," then mounted with cannon, and took possession of it, by surprise. This attack being unexpected, the attention of its defenders was drawn off, to view the scenes passing and events occurring at and near Towson's Battery, which was an unpardonable neglect of duty, for twenty five men could have effectually defended it from such an assault, had they been at their posts and on the alert. As soon as Colonel Drummond got into the Bastion, he cried, "Give the d—d Yankees no "quarters;" and what few Americans were in the Bastion, fled or were wantonly sacrificed, at which juncture a Lieutenant of the Artillery or Bombardier-corps, commander of a single gun, in an angle, in the parapet of the "Old "Fort," some fifteen or twenty yards distant from the Bastion, turned his gun alone, which was already loaded with grape-shot, towards the Bastion, and fired it, the effect of which was to set fire to a basket of cannon-cartridges, which had been placed, for the time being, under the plank-platform of the Bastion, in range with its entrance, at which the gun was pointed. The explosion of the cartridges in the basket blew up the Bastion floor, and scattered the materials of which its parapets were composed. This accident—for so it was considered, at the time, and it has never been asserted to the contrary, from any authentic source—therefore, I must say this accident ended the career of the vaunting Colonel Drummond, and killed or mortally wounded all the British who had taken possession of the Bastion and some who had not yet elevated themselves to that high distinction; but I believe the event is to be deplored by the Americans, as by it the brave officer who fired the cannon lost his life, and there were, probably, nearly as many Americans killed and wounded by the accident as there were British.

Of the truth of the facts above stated, in all their minutia, relative to the firing the gun by the officer, its direction, etc., we never had nor ever can have a living witness; but the fact of the gun, which had been previously loaded, being turned in the direction of the Bastion and fired; the basket of cartridges exploding at the same time; the commander of the gun being found dead at its breech, with no other marks of violence than those naturally produced by such an explosion; and no one claiming a participation in the deed, nor any other corpse being found, as a silent testimony of companionship, fully warrants us in coming to the conclusion of their undoubted truth, although the gun might have been pointed at the basket when fired, and its recoil produced a more elevated direction; yet such a conclusion is not probable; but if the gun was fired into the Bastion, the direction in which it was found, the wadding would have naturally fallen into the basket or its vicinity.

While Colonel Drummond and his Division made this attack on the Bastion, the third, and most numerous, Division made an attack on Douglass's Battery and our extreme right, where our Heavy Artillery, Bombardiers, and light-troops were posted. Douglass's Battery, under the direction of its then youthful but skilful and intrepid commander,* and the troops stationed in its vicinity, soon discomfited this Division, and compelled its crowded ranks to retreat beyond the reach of the shot from our guns.

Thus ended the assault on Fort Erie, in a complete failure; but the British prosecuted their siege, with renewed vigor, until the seventeenth of September, when a chivalrous sortie from the Fort compelled them to raise the siege and make a hasty retreat to Fort George, at the mouth of the Niagara-river.

That the explosion and destruction of the Bastion had any more effect on "the termina-'tion of the War," or even the capture of the Fort, than had the destruction of a camp washer-woman, by a random cannon-ball, is not to be entertained for a moment, for Colonel Drummond could not have retained possession, fifteen minutes, unless he was supported and sustained, from within the works, by the other two Divisions of the assailants, or, at least, by one of them; and they were both completely routed from their respective points of attack, before the explosion. Neither was the place where the basket of cartridges stood, the Magazine of the Fort, or even of the Bastion: it was, in fact, a very unsafe place to leave cartridges, on any occasion; and in this case they

* The late Major David B. Douglass, who died, a few years since, at Geneva, while filling a Professorship in Geneva College.

were undoubtedly hastily and carelessly left there. The Magazine of the Fort was in a compartment in the North end of the northern mess-house, near to, but disconnected with, the Bastion, which had no separate Magazine.

I can assure the public that I write understandingly, and from my own knowledge. as far as the nature of the case will admit. The facts and conclusions, herein stated, are not nursery chimeras or boyish phantasies. I was then a man, with an experience of twelve years in the scenes of manhood and active walks of life. Soon after the explosion, I visited Fort Erie and became an inmate of the tented field; and being personally acquainted with many of the Field, Staff, and Platoon-officers of our Army, and especially with Major, then Lieutenant, Douglass, who, with other officers, took me into the "Old Fort" and showed me the position of things as they were, at the time of the explosion, and related to me, in detail, the circumstances of that event, as far as they were known to the living—they deplored the fate of the young officer, who fired the gun, whose name I now forget, but made no allusion to his voluntary self-immolation.

I delineated, I presume, the first map or plan of the Fort, after the explosion, with explanatory notes and references and made several copies—General, then Colonel, Scott, on learning which, sent for me and solicited copies, one of which, as I understood, he sent to the War Department in Washington.

During the time I remained in the Fort, I heard soldiers relate divers marvellous accounts of the circumstances attending the blowing up of the Bastion, which were disregarded by the well-informed, as much as a sailor's long yarn is, by his Purser. One of these stories, I presume, has been the foundation of Mr. Daw's sincere belief; but, from any officer or well-informed person, I never heard of any kegs of powder being beneath the Bastion, or of any arrangements having been made to blow up the Magazine, on any emergency.

Yours, &c.,
EBENEZER MIX.

5.—REPLY TO MESSRS. DOUGLASS AND MIX, BY PROFESSOR WILSON.

[*From* The Buffalo Daily Courier, *Buffalo, November, 1853.*]

MR. SEAVER,
DEAR SIR: I do not suppose it possible for any one to misunderstand my object in sending to you the affidavit of Mr. Dow—not Daw, as it has been printed. It was to call out just such articles as that of the Rev. Mr. Douglass, in the *Courier* of the fourteenth instant, and

that of Mr. Mix, in the Batavia *Spirit of the Times*, of the fifteenth.

Although readily admitting all the ignorance of military affairs which these correspondents may be disposed to charge me with, I did not, however, possess enough to satisfy me that some of the points and statements of Mr. Dow were erroneous. Nor was I quite disposed to believe his story to be entirely a fabrication. The article of Mr. Mix, I think, furnishes the primary fact which was wrought up into story, as Dow has given it. He states that "a Lieu-"tenant of Artillery or Bombardier Corps, "commander of a single gun, in an angle in the "parapet," fired it; the effect of which was, to blow up the Bastion and kill himself in the act. Now I do not recollect any mention of this fact in Major Douglass's manuscript—though it may be there. But this fact is, in some measure, inconsistent with the Rev. Mr. Douglass's communication. For in that he says: "Major Douglass was the *only* Lieuten-"ant of Bombardiers in the action. Captain "Williams and Lieutenant McDonough, both "of the Artillery, are the *only* officers mention-"ed in General Gaines's Report as killed; *and* "*they were known to have been killed before the* "*Bastion was yielded to the enemy.*"

I hope we may hear yet further from those who had the means to know, and yet remember, the occurrences of that glorious night. It may be that we shall yet find reason to believe that the discharge of the gun was a noble act —though, perhaps, a mistake and unnecessary one—on the part of the Lieutenant who fired it.

Very sincerely, yours,
W. D. WILSON.

6.—LETTER FROM EBENEZER MIX, ESQR. TO REV. MALCOLM DOUGLASS.

[*From the original manuscript.*]

BATAVIA Nov. 14th 1853
REV. MALCOMB DOUGLAS,
DEAR SIR,

On perusing an account of the explosion of the bastion in old Fort Erie, in August 1814, I set down immediately and penned my views on the subject, but political matter crowded it out of the paper until this week, on leaving it I had directed a copy to be sent to you. This afternoon, while my reminiscences were issuing from the press, I came across the *Buffalo Courier*, containing your essay on the same subject—this evening I compared them—It could not have been expected that two men, had they both been within the fort (not to say "within the bastion") at the time, would after the lapse of 39 years, without previous concert, have told the history of such

an exciting event, nearer alike than we have done; although neither of us was present at the time & one of us unborn, we had however in a great measure, the same source of information, your lamented father, who was at that time & place, the chief engineer & had the superintendence of constructing all new works, and repairing & improving all the old works of the fort & encampment— We both discard the intention of impugning the veracity of Mr. Dow [not Daw] but both entirely dissent from the truth of his statement, in all its material points—we both give the same reason or cause for his errors, and attribute his statement to the same source—we agree that the occurrence was a mere accident, and deny, that there existed, among the officers any arrangements or preparations to blow up the magazine, on any contingency—We likewise agree on the effect, or rather non-effect which the explosion had on the termination of the war, or the capture of the fort, and we came to that conclusion predicated on the same facts— We substantially agree in assuming the circumstances and cause of the explosion— In one point, and I believe the only one, our statements do not co-incide, that is, whether there was, or was not a magazine under the bastion, the contents of which exploded, this may be thought to be a mere variance in phrasiologe, and that any place, where "some cart-"rages" had been lodged, whether safe or unsafe, however fortuitously or temporarily their deposit, was a magazine. but I think that every common reader as well as every military man, must conclude from your statement, that there was under the bastion something like a regular apartment for the lodgement & safe-keeping of combustible munitions of war and their concomitants— A mere sight of this place would refute the idea— Maj. Douglas says that it was "under the platform and quite "open" and I will add, as open as an old fashioned kitchen fire-place & about the size, without an apology for a door— But what says Gen. Gaines, the commanding officer at the time, in his report to the Secretary of War. "At this "moment every operation was arrested by the "explosion of *some cartridges* deposited at the "end of the stone building, adjoining the con-"tested bastion." By this statement it would be as hard to locate these "some cartriges" before the explosion as afterwards The Gen. was ashamed, and perhaps afraid to report to the Secretary, that it was the explosion of a corn basket of cartrages tucked under the floor of the bastion!—neither would he report that it was the explosion of "some cartrages" in the magazine of the fort or bastion, for that would not have been the truth—therefore he made this evasive or to say the most of it, indefinite statement; this might have passed as immaterial had not Mr. Dow lugged his 20 kegs of powder into it.

As to the person who fired off the gun, there is no particular discrepancy in our statements —I should have said—" An artillery officer who "had charge of the single gun &c." and so I wrote it in my first draft, his grade or whether a commissioned officer or not I did not recollect, but not wishing to contradict Mr. Dow's statement unnecessarily, I introduced the words, "Lieut." & "bombardier" But I am very certain, that several officers of the higher grade, and Maj. Douglas, in particular, while on the ground, viewing the premises, a few days after the explosion, told his friend, D. E. Evans & myself that according to the best testimony to be obtained, as there was no living witness,— the officer commanding the single gun at the angle, turned the gun alone, already charged with grape-shot, and fired into the bastion, and that the wad or some other ignited substance from the charge, fell into the basket of cartrages beneath the platform, on which the explosion took place.

I have just viewed a second bulletin from Prof. Wilson, through the *Buffalo Courier*, in which he accuses *us* of charging him with ignorance in military affairs—he should have charged *me* only—I however did not intend to offend him—but when I found a Professor in such an institution as Geneva College, speak of "making a *sortie* on a Fort," instead of a *charge*, and using several other very clumsy expressions, when addressing the public, I could not resist giving him a rap over the knuckles, but I did it without exposing his defects, or rather the defects in his writing- People who write to the public, should be prepared to meet criticism.

I insert herein a rough plan of Old Fort Eric, and some of its annexed works by the Americans. I do not however do it for your edification, as I presume you have far better drawings of it among your fathers papers, this plan and its explanatory references are mostly copied from your fathers drawings, but I send this to you to let you understand how I conceive the facts to be- *

Yours very Respectfully
EBENEZER MIX

P. S. Your friend Wilson, in his last bulletin says that, he "did not however possess "enough [ignorance] to satisfy him that *some* "of the points and statements of Mr. Dow "were erroneous, nor was I [Wilson] quite dis-

* It has not been considered necessary to re-produce this map, because it is almost exactly a copy of that which we have given on another page.—EDITOR.

"posed to believe his story to be ⬛⬛⬛ a "fabrication." [A curious sentence, ⬛⬛ ⬛⬛ly put together—my opinion is that ⬛⬛ ⬛⬛ cannot write elegantly or even ordinarily, if these two efforts are good specimens]

Mr. Dow with Mr. W. to back him, I think comes out about as well as the old indian who having sold a deer, which he had just killed and left hanging in a certain tree in a certain meadow, as he said—and no deer being found there—he was upbraided by the purchaser for lying and replied— You found the meadow— Yes- You found the tree—Yes- And you found the deer—No- Hugh, two *trutes* to one lie—pretty good for indian! The fort was there & the bastion was blown up—all the rest of " his story " appears " to be entirely a fabri-"cation "

If Mr. Wilson calls me out again I will fire off my big Gun at him.

IV.—KINDERHOOK, NEW YORK.

[The following articles, concerning this ancient town, are taken from a local newspaper, in order that they may not be lost, among the transient items of weekly journals. They are evidently from the pen of our friend, Henry C. Van Schaack, Esqr., of Manlius, New York, who is a native of Kinderhook; and, as they are perfectly reliable, we have pleasure in re-printing them.—EDITOR.]

I.

NATURAL HISTORY OF KINDERHOOK.

To THE EDITOR OF THE ADVERTISER:

In the early part of the present century, a communication appeared in *The Balance and Columbia Repository*, a newspaper then published at Hudson, containing observations on the natural history of the village of Kinderhook and its vicinity. The author of this paper was the Rev. David B. Warden, who was a resident of this village, for several years, during the tenth decade of the last century. He was the Principal of the first Academy established here; and afterwards became Principal of the Academy, at Kingston, in this State. When General Armstrong was our Minister in France, Mr. Warden was Secretary of Legation; and he was subsequently appointed Consul, which latter office he held for many years. He is represented to have been a man of deep and varied learning, of which there is some evidence in the fact that, while in Paris, he was made a member of the noted French Academy. His death occurred in that city, many years ago, at the age of sixtyeight. His library, said to possess historical value, was purchased from him, in his lifetime, by the State of New York. As the observations of an intelligent foreigner, for Mr. Warden was an Englishman, it is believed that his communi-